CHEKHOV ON WRITING

The Mentor, The Self-Critic, Literary
Questions and Fictional Writers

CHEKHOV ON WRITING
The Mentor, The Self-Critic, Literary Questions and Fictional Writers

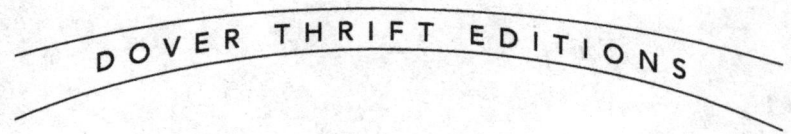

DOVER THRIFT EDITIONS

Anton Chekhov

Edited by
Bob Blaisdell

DOVER PUBLICATIONS
GARDEN CITY, NEW YORK

DOVER THRIFT EDITIONS

GENERAL EDITOR: SUSAN L. RATTINER
EDITOR OF THIS VOLUME: MICHAEL CROLAND

Chekhov on Writing: The Mentor, The Self-Critic, Literary Questions and Fictional Writers is a new work, first published by Dover Publications in 2025.

ISBN-13: 978-0-486-85460-1
ISBN-10: 0-486-85460-4

Printed in the United States of America
85460401   2025
www.doverpublications.com

I dedicate this book to the teacher, mentor, and friend who introduced me to Chekhov, the author Max Schott. In his literary advice, he has been as generous to me and his other students as Chekhov was to *his* "pupils."

Contents

Contents

Introduction

Don't invent sufferings you have not experienced, and don't paint
pictures you have not seen—for a lie in a story is much more boring
than a lie in conversation.
—Letter to his brother Aleksandr, April 6, 1886

MANY READERS HAVE found that Anton Pavlovich Chekhov (1860–
1904) is the easiest to warm to among the great nineteenth-century
Russian authors. In contrast to Fyodor Dostoyevsky and Leo Tolstoy,
for instance, his art is modest, decidedly not grand, primarily appearing
in the form of short stories and novellas and a handful of domestic
dramas. Biographically, he was also modest. He was not an aristocrat
but rather the son of a former serf. He was funny, demonstrably kind,
and generous. He was a doctor and the breadwinner for his parents and
siblings. He was immensely popular among a wide range of Russian
readers. He did not marry until he was forty-one and slowly dying
of tuberculosis. He was born and grew up in the southern port town of
Taganrog, where his father, Pavel—whose own tyrannical and clever
father had bought his family out of serfdom—ran a general store,
staffed by his older sons. Chekhov was the third child out of six.
When the store went bankrupt in 1876, Pavel and his wife and other
children fled creditors and went to Moscow, where Chekhov's two
older brothers were studying. Chekhov was left in Taganrog to finish high school. In 1879, he won a local scholarship to study at a
university in Moscow, and that fall, he rejoined his family.

As a medical student, Chekhov began publishing short stories and
skits in humor magazines. Through the fees he collected for his
writings, he was soon supporting his parents and three younger siblings.
His self-discipline led to him becoming the de facto head of the

family. Certified as a doctor in 1884, he realized he could more easily earn a living as a writer than as a general practitioner. Eventually, his medical practice was pro bono for all. From 1880 to 1885, he published hundreds of stories, articles, and other pieces under various comical pseudonyms. Indeed, Antosha Chekhonte became famous in his own right as the most popular writer in the St. Petersburg humor magazine *Fragments*. When asked to contribute longer and serious stories to the literary section of the prominent St. Petersburg newspaper *New Times* in January 1886, the editor, Aleksei Suvorin, insisted that Chekhov use his real name. Chekhov balked at first, as he had wanted to preserve "Anton Chekhov for future medical and scientific articles." Relenting, he fully became the beloved Anton Chekhov to the expanding Russian reading public as well as to the era's most esteemed authors, among them Tolstoy and Nikolai Leskov, who enthusiastically admired him.

Through 1887, he published more than a short story a week. By 1888, he slowed down his pace to that of a normal, productive writer. He was already reading and critiquing drafts of stories from anyone who asked him. Once he sensed a correspondent's seriousness to accept criticism, he offered it with the entirety of his artistic sensibility. There has never been an author of his stature who was as open to giving away candid detailed advice to budding writers.[1] "I am at home to all commencing, continuing, and concluding authors—that is my rule," he told eighteen-year-old Elena Shavrova.[2]

★

I have sorted Chekhov's thoughts on and representations of writing into four categories, with each section laid out chronologically. The first, "The Mentor," contains his candid, critical, and generous assessments of his friends' and acquaintances' stories and plays. These were almost always requested critiques. He insisted on rules for his correspondents that he was constantly applying to himself:

> [. . .] when you depict sad or unlucky people, and want to touch the reader's heart, try to be colder—it gives their grief as it were a background,

---

[1] My conscience prompts me to think of one more: the American poet Ezra Pound (1885–1972), who, despite his treasonous and anti-Semitic insanity, was for decades a brilliant literary advisor to almost all-comers. See, for instance, *The Selected Letters of Ezra Pound: 1907–1941* (New Directions).

[2] Letter of November 19, 1891. [Translation by Louis S. Friedland.]

against which it stands out in greater relief. As it is, your heroes weep and you sigh. Yes, you must be cold.[3]

The only person to whom Chekhov was regularly impatient in these quotations was his talented older brother Aleksandr. Although Aleksandr had published humorous stories before Anton had, he did not have Anton's practical sensibility or, more importantly, his sobriety and ethics. "My holy of holies," declared Chekhov to an editor, "is the human body, health, intelligence, talent, inspiration, love, and the most absolute freedom—freedom from violence and lying, whatever forms they may take."[4] Even as a twenty-three-year-old, Anton was laying out for Aleksandr commonsense rules for writing for *Fragments*. Among those rules: "the shorter the better." In his informal but sharp advice, we also learn something profound about Chekhov's own fiction. In 1889, annoyed with Aleksandr's artistic backsliding, he asked, "Is there no life outside of you? And who is interested in knowing my life or yours, my thoughts and your thoughts? Give people people, and not yourself."[5] Chekhov insisted that even if he had shared many of his own experiences with those of his characters, he did not write autobiographically. His most revealing statement on that topic was to his friend Ivan Leont'ev: "You should never describe yourself. It would have been better had you made Pospelov fall in love with some woman, and incorporated your feelings in her."[6]

As penetrating as his criticisms were, Chekhov was careful to remind his correspondents to be leery of them: "It happens that I have been mistaken quite often, and I have held other opinions than those I have just expressed. On occasion my criticism has proved worthless."[7]

The second section, "The Self-Critic," is where Chekhov directs his analysis to his own work and methods. He is more serious, more critical, less forgiving, and quite a bit less generous about his work, yet he is always interesting and usually amusing. Because he was occupied in his late twenties as much with his medical practice as

---

[3] Letter of March 19, 1892, to Lidia Avilova. [LF]
[4] Letter of October 4, 1888, to the editor Aleksandr Pleshcheev. [Translation by Louis S. Friedland, who mistakenly attributed the letter as being addressed to Aleksei Suvorin. See Chekhov's *Collected Works* in Russian.]
[5] Letter of May 8, 1889. [LF]
[6] Letter of February 2, 1888. [LF]
[7] Letter of January 22, 1888, to Ivan Leont'ev (Shcheglov). [LF]

with his writing, he reflected on this "problem" to his friend, the
New Times editor Suvorin:

> You advise me not to hunt after two hares, and not to think of med-
> ical work. I do not know why one should not hunt two hares even
> in the literal sense. I feel more confident and more satisfied with myself
> when I reflect that I have two professions and not one. Medicine is
> my lawful wife and literature is my mistress. When I get tired of one
> I spend the night with the other. Though it's disorderly, it's not so
> dull, and besides, neither of them loses anything from my infidelity.
> If I did not have my medical work I doubt if I could have given my
> leisure and my spare thoughts to literature.

He added, to what must have been Suvorin's reasonable disbelief:
"There is no discipline in me."[8]

The third section, "Literary Questions," is made up of his discussions or debates with his friends about the purposes and limitations
of artistic productions. "I agree that 'pearls' are a good thing," he
rebutted Maria Kiseleva, "but then a writer is not a confectioner,
not a provider of cosmetics, not an entertainer; he is a man bound,
under contract, by his sense of duty and his conscience; having put
his hand to the plow he mustn't turn back, and, however distasteful,
he must conquer his squeamishness and soil his imagination with the
dirt of life."[9]

The final section, "Fictional Writers," includes excerpts from his
stories and the play *The Seagull*, in which he dramatizes, usually
comically, various fictitious authors' daily lives and their struggles
in composing their writings. In one of his finest stories, "Easter Eve,"
Chekhov's narrator listens to an admirer of a recently deceased monk
who wrote "hymns of praise." The admirer sees in such writing the
qualities that Chekhov strove for in his own work: "Everything must
be harmonious, brief and complete."

---

[8] Letter of September 11, 1888. [LF]
[9] Letter of January 14, 1887. [Translation by Constance Garnett.]

I.

THE MENTOR

Aleksandr Chekhov, the oldest Chekhov sibling, was a writer and editor.

NIKOLAI [THE SECOND of five Chekhov brothers] has just given me your letter to read. The question about the right to read or not to read must be laid aside for lack of time. [. . .] Unluckily, I have not the time to write all that I should. For the sake of good form and proper exposition I'll have recourse to a framework, to a system: I shall proceed to analyze your letter by stages from A to Z inclusive. I am the critic; your letter is the work which is interesting from the artistic standpoint. As one who has read it, I have the right to criticize. Just consider yourself as the author—and all will go famously. [. . .]

You are an excellent stylist; you have read a lot, written a lot; you understand things as well as others and it's nothing to you to write a kind word to your brother. Not a sermon—never! But if instead of shedding tears you would talk to him about his painting, he for certain would sit down to his work straight away and be sure to answer you. You know how he can be influenced.

"But I am forgetting myself. This is my final letter to you." All that is nonsense; the point is not in that. That is not what needs emphasis. You, the strong one, educated and well read, should emphasize what is vital, what is eternal, what affects not only petty feelings but true human sensibilities. You are capable of doing this. Of course you are! You are witty, a realist, an artist. For that letter of yours in which you describe divine service in a forest clearing I would, if I were God, forgive you all your trespasses, voluntary and involuntary, in deed and in word. (Nikolai, by the way, reading that letter had a terrible desire to paint that field.) But even in your writing you

1

lay too much stress upon trivial things. And you were not born a subjective writer.

That kind of writing is not inborn in one; it is acquired. It is as easy to give up that self-acquired subjectivity as to drink a glass of water. One needs only to be a bit more honest; to throw oneself absolutely overboard, not to push oneself as the hero of one's novel, to deny oneself for even half an hour. There is a story of yours where a young couple sit kissing each other all through dinner, sitting and cooing and talking rubbish. There's not a single sensible word, but thorough complacency. And you were not writing for the reader. You wrote because that chatter pleased you. Why don't you describe the dinner—how they ate, what they ate, what the cook was like, how vulgar your hero was, how satisfied with his lazy contentment, how vulgar your heroine, how ridiculous her love for that smug, napkinned, overfed gander? Everyone likes to see well-fed, happy people—that's true. But if you are going to write about them it's not enough to tell what they said and the number of times they kissed. A something else is needed. You must deny yourself the personal impression that honeymoon happiness produces on all unembittered persons. Subjectivity is an awful thing—even for the reason that it betrays the poor writer hand over fist. I bet you that all the vicars' daughters and clerks' wives who read your writings are in love with you; and were you a German you would drink beer gratis in all the beer-shops where there are German barmaids.

If only you would give up that subjectivity you would become a most useful writer. You know so well how to laugh, to bite, to sneer; you have such a well-rounded style; you have experienced so much, and seen more than enough. Ah! material is being thrown away. You might at least put some of it in your letters and encourage Nikolai's imagination thereby. [. . .]
—to Aleksandr Chekhov, February 20, 1883 [SK-1]

★

Write stories of about 50–80 lines, trifles, and so on [for *Fragments* magazine] . . . . Send five or ten little stories at a time. They will be published at once. The fee is excellent and prompt. Send to Petersburg direct. The chief thing is: (1) the shorter the better; (2) a little idea, topical, *à propos*; (3) a little buffoonery is all right, but ignorance of rank and of the seasons is forbidden.
—to Aleksandr Chekhov, April 17–18, 1883 [SK-1]

★

Why do you write so little? How disgusting! [. . .] All the stories you sent me for Leikin smell strongly of idleness. [. . .] Respect yourself, for the love of Christ; don't give your hands liberty when your brain is lazy! Write no more than two stories a week, shorten them, polish them. Work should be work. Don't invent sufferings you have not experienced, and don't paint pictures you have not seen—for a lie in a story is much more boring than a lie in conversation. . . .

Remember every minute that you will need your pen and your talent in the future more than you do now, so don't profane them . . .

[. . .] Literature has been no labor to you, but most surely it is labor. Were you a decent man, were you to sit at a story (of 150 or 200 lines) for five or seven days, what a result there would be! You would not recognize yourself in your lines, just as you don't recognize yourself in the mirror. . . . Consider, you are not piled up with pressing work, and therefore you can work on one little thing for several evenings. Is it profitable? Count. With great minuteness you could write five or seven stories a month, which would make about a hundred rubles; and now, though you write a great deal, you don't make fifty. [. . .]

Do remember, now: work on your stories. I can judge by experience. Write.
—to Aleksandr Chekhov, April 6, 1886 [SK-1]

★

[Your story] "The City of the Future" will become an artistic production only by the following conditions: 1) the absence of prolix wordy politico-socialistic-economic features; 2) continuous objectivity; 3) correctness in describing people and objects; 4) special brevity; 5) boldness and originality; fleeing from stereotypes; 6) heart.
—Aleksandr Chekhov, May 10, 1886 [BB]

★

In my opinion a true description of Nature should be very brief and have a character of relevance. Commonplaces such as "the setting sun bathing in the waves of the darkening sea poured its purple gold, etc."; "the swallows flying over the surface of the water twittered merrily"; such commonplaces one ought to abandon. In descriptions

of Nature one ought to seize upon the little particulars, grouping
them in such a way that, in reading, when you shut your eyes, you
get a picture.

For instance, you will get the full effect of a moonlight night if
you write that on the mill-dam a little glowing star-point flashed
from the neck of a broken bottle, and the round, black shadow of a
dog, or a wolf, emerged and ran, etc.[10] Nature becomes animated
if you are not squeamish about employing comparisons of her
phenomena with ordinary human activities, etc.

In the sphere of psychology, details are also the thing. God preserve
us from commonplaces. Best of all is it to avoid depicting the
hero's state of mind; you ought to try to make it clear from the hero's
actions. It is not necessary to portray many characters. The center of
gravity should be in two persons: him and her.

I write this to you as a reader having a definite taste. Also, in order
that you, when writing, may not feel alone. To be alone in work is
a hard thing. Better poor criticism than none at all. Is it not so?
—to Aleksandr Chekhov, May 10, 1886 [LF]

★

*Maria Kiseleva's family owned the Babkino estate, where Chekhov rented a
dacha for his family each summer from 1885 to 1887. About a dozen years
older than Chekhov, she was a mother and an aspiring children's book author.
He helped her publish several stories. Although Kiseleva and Chekhov were
fond of each other and enjoyed fishing together, they often squabbled over literary issues.*

Of course, there is no need to assure you that I'm very glad to be
your literary-agent, retailer and guide. This duty flatters my vanity
and fulfilling it will be as easy as carrying a pail for you when you
return from fishing. If you have to know my conditions, take these:

1. Write as much as possible! Write, write, write . . . until your
   fingers are broken. (The main thing in life—penmanship!) Write
   more, having in view not so much the intelligent development
   of the big parts as much as the details, so that at first a fair half of
   your skits, due to your being unaccustomed to the "small press,"

---

[10] Chekhov's example is a paraphrase from his short story "Hydrophobia" (published
March 17, 1886).

will be rejected. As for receiving rejections, I am not going to deceive you, be hypocritical or lie—I give you my word. But don't let the rejections bother you. Even if half will receive rejections, then the work will be more profitable than the Bohemian's in *Children's Recreation*. But as for self-esteem . . . I don't know about you, but I've been used to it a long time.

2. Write on various themes, funny and tearful, good and bad. Do stories, sketches, jokes, witticisms, puns and so on and so forth.

3. Adaptations from foreign work—the thing is fully legal, but only in the case if your sins against the 8th Commandment don't poke you in your eyes . . . (For "Galoshes" you're going to Hell after the 22nd of January!) Flee from popular subjects. As stupid as our editors are, exposing their ignorance of Parisian literature, especially Maupassant's, is not easy work.

4. Write in one sitting, with full belief in your pen. Honestly, I'm not speaking hypocritically: eight-tenths of the writers of the "small press" in comparison with you are shoemakers and losers.

5. Brevity is recognized in the small press as the first virtue. The best measure would be to work on stationery (the same as that which I'm writing on). As soon as you get 8–10 pages, like so—stop! And the stationery is easier to send . . . Those are all my conditions.

—to Maria Kiseleva, September 29, 1886 [BB]

★

1. "Galoshes" lies on my table and will be put into circulation only after the New Year, in a shortened, corrected way. It's necessary to flush from it the French smell, otherwise it will come out like an adaptation, and that is no good and unfitting; as a novice it's always better to begin with the original. If your first story is "too busy," all the following ones will be seen with prejudice.

2. The story about the madwoman, titled by me "Who's Happier?" is a very sweet, warm and gracious story. Even the dog Leikin, not knowing anybody besides Turgenev and me, found that this story is "not-bad and literary." (Not wanting to be the sole judge, I brought it for advice to Leikin and other old literary dogs.) The most successful place for me—*Petersburg Gazette*, but alas! Because of the fee I broke off from that periodical (I'm demanding a raise). In *Fragments* it's impossible to place, as it's not humorous. The only thing remaining—wait for it in *The Alarm Clock*, where in its feuilleton-pages

they publish "serious" studies (for example, my "Oysters"), which I did. So, your story will be published in *The Alarm Clock*. Thanks to the idiotic manner of journals to mix up signed things, belonging to "names," that is, firms (Zlatovratski, Nefedov, Chekhov and such representatives of the fall of contemporary literature), your story will be placed not in the near future. But for you this is indifferent, as the money can be had before publication. [. . .]

We need to talk over many things. So, I have to justify some corrections in your stories . . . For example in "Who's Happier?" the beginning is pretty bad . . . It's a dramatic story, but you begin with "shooting himself" in a humorous tone. Then the "hysterical laughter" is a much too old effect . . . The simpler the movements the more plausible and sincere, and therefore better . . . In "Galoshes" there are many mistakes of such kind as "House No. 49." In Moscow there is no numbering of addresses . . . Turning to the last story, by memory by the way, that Lentovsky is completely out of place. He is very much not as popular in Moscow as Aleksei Sergeevich [Suvorin], who for some reason loves him.

—to Maria Kiseleva, October 29, 1886 [BB]

*

You might write a sketch, "Ivan Gavrilov," or "The Wounded Doe." In the latter story, if you have not forgotten, the hunters wound the doe which looks at them like a human being, and nobody can make up his mind to kill her. This is not a bad subject, but dangerous in the sense that it is hard to escape sentimentality; you ought to write it like a protocol, without pitying words, and begin thus, "On such and such a date, some hunters wounded a young elk in the Daraganov forest" . . . But if you let fall a tear or two, you will rob the subject of its austerity and of all that is worthy of attention.

—to Maria Kiseleva, December 3, 1886 [LF]

*

Forgive me, I so like your story that I am ready to write you a dozen sheets, though I know I can tell you nothing new or good. . . . I restrain myself and am silent, fearing to bore you and to say something silly. I will say once more that your story is magnificent. [. . .] Hard as I tried I could detect only two small blots; even those are rather farfetched! (1) the characteristics of the people interrupt the

picture of the dream and give the impression of explanation notes, which in gardens botanists nail on trees and spoil the scenery; (2) at the beginning of the story the feeling of cold is soon blunted in the reader and becomes too usual, owing to the frequent repetition of the word "cold."
—to Dmitri Grigorovich, February 12, 1887 [CG]

★

You, as the groomsman of my *Ivanov*, I regard it as not out of place to communicate the following: *Ivanov* will definitely go on at the end of November or early December. From this comes the moral: "Don't be shy, young people!"

Of course it's bad that you're lazy and write little. You're a "beginner" in the full meaning of that word and ought not to forget under the fear of a death sentence that each line in the present establishes capital for the future. If now you don't train your hand and your head to discipline and forced marches, if you don't hurry and tune yourself, in 3–4 years it will be already too late. You [and Aleksandr Lazarev-Gruzinsky] both work too little. [. . .] For example, my brother Agafopod[11] wrote meagerly and now already feels written out. . . . You know that whoever's a little and lazy cockroach begins impotence early. I say this to you on a scientific basis.
—to Nikolai Ezhov, October 27, 1887 [BB]

★

You don't so much need to be praised for writing well as to be scolded and vilified for how little you write. . . . In "Mignon," which was nice, I found several blunders that I explained to myself only by your writing too little. Ignite yourself! After all, you take fire so easily! "Writing too little is as dangerous for one who writes as the absence of practice is for a man of medicine" (Socrates, X.v.[12]).
—to Ivan Leont'ev (Shcheglov), January 10, 1888 [BB]

★

---

[11] Agafopod is just one of Chekhov's nicknames for his brother Aleksandr.
[12] This is Chekhov's tongue-in-cheek reference.

Oh you of little faith, you are interested to know what flaws I found in your "Mignon." Before I point them out I warn you that they have a technical rather than a critico-literary interest. Only a writer can appreciate them, but a reader not at all. Here they are. . . . I think that you, an author scrupulous and untrusting, afraid that your characters will not stand out clearly enough, are too much given to thoroughly detailed description. The result is an overwrought "motleyness" of effect that impairs the general impression.

In order to show how powerfully music can affect one at times, but distrustful of the reader's ability to understand you readily, you zealously set forth the psychology of your Feodrik; the psychology is successful, but then the interval between two such moments as "amare, morire" [Italian: "love, die"] and the pistol-shot, is dragged out unduly, and the reader, before he reaches the suicide-scene, has had time to recover from the pain of "amare, morire." But you must give the reader no chance to recover: he must always be kept in suspense. These remarks would not apply if "Mignon" were a novel. Long, detailed works have their own peculiar aims, which require a most careful execution regardless of the total impression. But in short stories it is better to say not enough than to say too much, because— because—I don't know why! At all events, remember that your failings are considered flaws only by myself (altogether unimportant flaws), and I am very often mistaken. Perhaps you are right and not I. . . . It happens that I have been mistaken quite often, and I have held other opinions than those I have just expressed. On occasion my criticism has proved worthless.

—to Ivan Leont'ev (Shcheglov), January 22, 1888 [LF]

*

You are a good writer, but you lack entirely the ability or the desire to look objectively at things. Nerves, nerves, and nerves again! Byezhetsky does not speak well of your "Mignon"? That is to be expected. Writers are as jealous as pigeons. Leikin is put out if some other writer turns his attention to the life of the merchant-class; Leskov hates to read novels from priests' life not written by himself; and Byezhetsky will never acknowledge your military sketches because he regards himself as the sole specialist in the military field. And you do not care for his wonderful "The Soldiers in the War." Everybody is highly strung and jealous.

You claim that Burenin is embittered against you. Like most writers he seldom expresses a favorable opinion behind one's back, but should someone ask him whom he regards with greater esteem— you, or Salias whom he praises—he would laugh at the humor of the question.

If you could bring yourself to look upon life objectively you would cease to sing the tune of Lazarus. You are one of the happiest of modern writers. Everybody reads you, is pleased, praises you, elects you to "membership," your plays are produced and are well attended. . . . What do you require of the Muses? In literature you already hold the rank of major (with gold stripes), and this rank should be the charm to keep you from fear and from losing hope of the future because of some stinging fleas and a dog howling beneath the window.
—to Ivan Leont'ev (Shcheglov), February 4, 1888 [LF]

★

[The character] Pospelov is touching; he is an ideal man and a hero. Unfortunately, you are subjective to the last degree. You should never describe yourself. It would have been better had you made Pospelov fall in love with some woman, and incorporated your feelings in her.
—to Ivan Leont'ev (Shcheglov), February 22, 1888 [LF]

★

Your chief merit in the longer works is the absence of pretension, and the vivid, natural dialogue. Your chief fault—you like to repeat yourself, . . . so that the reader becomes somewhat tired. Then another merit—the simpler the plot the better, and your plots are simple, taken from life, and not affected. In your place I should write a short novel based on tradesmen's life . . . I would describe ordinary love and family life without villains and angels, without lawyers and she-devils. I would take as my subject the even, smooth, ordinary life as it actually is, and I would depict "merchant happiness." . . . The life of the Russian tradesman is more purposeful, useful, wise, and typical than the life of the pathetic, vain-glorious men of Al'bov, Barantsevich, Muravlin, etc. However, I'm babbling.
—to Nikolai Leikin, May 11, 1888 [LF]

★

Every dramatist (the professional which you wish to be), must count on eight unsuccessful plays out of every ten. Every dramatist has to bear misfortunes that sometimes last for years, and he must be powerful enough to contend against these.
—to Ivan Leont'ev (Shcheglov), June 9, 1888 [LF]

★

Send me "The Theater Bird." You are a brave and clever chap to have written a comedy. Write at full speed, and in any manner you are moved to at the given moment. Should you be inspired to write a tragedy—write; if, on the other hand, the mood dictates a light farce—write that. Your nature cannot adapt itself to the views and rules laid down by someone else. You must follow your own inner feeling; this is the best indicator for nervous and sensitive people. And the plays you write will be the better for it. Oh, I've fallen again into moralizing!
—to Ivan Leont'ev (Shcheglov), July 18, 1888 [LF]

★

Your descriptions of nature aren't bad; you do well to fear trivialities and conventionality. But then again, you aren't giving your temperament free rein. For that reason, your techniques have no originality. You need to describe women so that the reader feels that you are sitting there in an unbuttoned waistcoat with no tie. And the same with nature. Give yourself freedom.
—to Aleksandr Lazarev-Gruzinsky, October 20, 1888 [BB]

★

Try to be original in your play and as clever as possible; but don't be afraid to show yourself foolish; we must have freedom of thinking, and only he is an emancipated thinker who is not afraid to write foolish things. Don't round things out, don't polish but be awkward and impudent. Brevity is the sister of talent. Remember, by the way, that declarations of love, the infidelity of husbands and wives; widows, orphans, and all other tears have long since been written up. The subject ought to be new, but there need be no "fable." And the main thing is: father and mother must eat. Write.
—Aleksandr Chekhov, April 11, 1889 [LF]

★

Now about your play. You undertook to depict a man who has not a grief in the world, and then you took fright. The problem seems to me to be clear. Only he has no grief who is indifferent; and people who are indifferent and aloof are either philosophers or petty, egotistic natures. The latter should be treated negatively, the former, positively. Of course those unmoved dullards who will suffer no pain even when you burn them with red-hot irons, they cannot be discussed at all. Even if by a man without grief you understand one who is not indifferent to the life about him, and who bravely and patiently bears the blows of fate, and looks hopefully to the future, there, too, the problem is comparatively simple and clear.

The large number of revisions need not trouble you, for the more of a mosaic the work is, the better. The characters stand to gain by this. The play will be worthless if all the characters resemble you. In this respect your "Money-Box" is monotonous and arouses a feeling of boredom. What are Natasha, Kolya, Tosya for? Is there no life outside of you? And who is interested in knowing my life or yours, my thoughts and your thoughts? Give people people, and not yourself.

Avoid "choice" diction. The language should be simple and forceful. The lackeys should speak simply, without elegance. Retired captains in the reserve, with huge, red noses, newspaper-reporters who drink, starving authors, consumptive women-toilers, honest young people without a flaw in their make-up, ideal maidens, good-natured nurses—all these have been described again and again, and should be avoided as a pitfall. Still another suggestion: go to the theater now and then and watch the stage. Compare, that is important. The first act may last as long as a whole hour, but the rest should not be more than twenty minutes each. The crux of a play is the third act, but it must not be so strong a climax as to kill the last act.
—to Aleksandr Chekhov, May 8, 1889 [LF]

★

I received your farce and read it through in no time. It's written beautifully, but its architecture is intolerable. It's completely unsuited to the stage. Judge for yourself. Dasha's first monologue is absolutely unnecessary; it sticks out like a sore thumb. It would be appropriate if you wanted to make Dasha not simply a walk-on part, and if it (the monologue) held great promise for the spectator, had some kind of relationship to the play's contents or effects. You can't put a loaded rifle on the stage if no one is intending to fire it. You can't promise. Let Dasha be completely silent—it's better that way. [. . .]

Such is my opinion. I will await your letter. Choose whichever way: either I will pass on the play in its present form—it might come off as is, since it is better than a hundred farces, or I will send it back to you for revisions.
—to Aleksandr Lazarev-Gruzinsky, November 1, 1889 [BB]

★

Elena Shavrova was fifteen years old in 1889 when she met Chekhov and asked for his criticism of one of her stories. A few years later, she became a devoted correspondent and pupil. He offered several more pieces of requested advice over the years. With Chekhov's guidance, she published six stories in Suvorin's New Times.

Well, if you need an actor, why not take an actual one, for example, Lensky, and not that wax, saint-like figure? I can't bear two-legged gods, especially if they are invented. Give us life!
—to Elena Shavrova, March 6, 1891 [LF]

★

You express disappointment that your story is uninteresting. Let me tell you that if only one of your five stories has the power to entertain the reader, you may thank God for that. It is not the writing of uninteresting attempts that is terrible, but it is terrible when one feels it a boring task to write, and hateful tedium. . . .
—to Elena Shavrova, June 20, 1891 [LF]

★

So we old bachelors smell of dogs? So be it. But as for specialists in feminine diseases being at heart rakes and cynics, allow me to differ. Gynecologists have to do with deadly prose such as you have never dreamed of, and to which perhaps, if you knew it, you would, with the ferocity characteristic of your imagination, attribute a worse smell than that of dogs. One who is always swimming in the sea loves dry land; one who forever is plunged in prose passionately longs for poetry. All gynecologists are idealists. Your doctor reads poems, your instinct prompted you right; I would add that he is a great liberal, a bit of a mystic, and that he dreams of a wife in the style of the Nekrasov Russian woman. The famous Snegirev cannot speak of the "Russian woman" without a quiver in his voice. Another gynecologist whom I know is in love with a mysterious lady in a veil whom he has seen only from a distance. Another goes to all the first performances at the theater and then is loud in his abuse, declaring that authors ought to represent only ideal women, and so on.

You have omitted to consider also that a good gynecologist cannot be a stupid man or a mediocrity. Intellect has a brighter luster than baldness, but you have noticed the baldness and emphasized it—and have flung the intellect overboard. You have noticed, too, and emphasized that a fat man—*brrr!*—exudes a sort of greasiness, but you completely lose sight of the fact that he is a professor—that is, that he has spent several years in thinking and doing something which sets him high above millions of men, high above all the Verochkas and Taganrog Greek girls, high above dinners and wines of all sorts.

Noah had three sons, Shem, Ham, and Japhet. Ham noticed only that his father was a drunkard, and completely lost sight of the fact that he was a genius, that he had built an ark and saved the world. Writers must not imitate Ham, bear that in mind.

I do not venture to ask you to love the gynecologist and the professor, but I venture to remind you of the justice which for an objective writer is more precious than the air he breathes. The girl of the merchant class is admirably drawn. That is a good passage in the doctor's speech in which he speaks of his lack of faith in medicine, but there is no need to make him drink after every sentence. Love for a corpse?—this is a rattling of your captive thoughts. You've not seen corpses.

Then from the particular to the general. Let me warn you. This is not a story and not a novel and not a work of art, but a long row of heavy, gloomy barracks buildings. Where is your construction which at first so enchanted your humble servant? Where is the lightness, the freshness, the grace? Read your story through: a description of a dinner, then a description of passing ladies and girls, then a description of a company, then a description of a dinner . . . and so on endlessly. Descriptions and descriptions and no action at all. You ought to begin straight away with the merchant's daughter, and keep

to her, and throw out Verochka and the Greek girls and all the rest, except the doctor and the merchant family
—to Elena Shavrova, September 16, 1891 [LF]

★

I am at home to all commencing, continuing, and concluding authors—that is my rule, and apart from your authorship and mine, I regard a visit from you as a great honor to me. [. . .]

But can you really have written only fifteen stories?—at this rate you won't learn to write till you are fifty. Write another twenty stories and send them. I shall always read them with pleasure, and practice is essential for you.
—to Elena Shavrova, November 19, 1891 [LF]

★

I have read your story "On the Road." If I were the editor of an illustrated magazine, I should publish the story with great pleasure; but here is my advice as a reader: when you depict sad or unlucky people, and want to touch the reader's heart, try to be colder—it gives their grief as it were a background, against which it stands out in greater relief. As it is, your heroes weep and you sigh. Yes, you must be cold.

But don't listen to me, I am a bad critic. I have not the faculty of forming my critical ideas clearly. Sometimes I make a regular hash of it.
—to Lidia Avilova, March 19, 1892 [LF]

★

I could not suggest a better medicine against moodiness and depression than writing plays and novels. It means quiet, painstaking, and interesting work, largely because one does not deal with lay figures and with politics, but with people whom one chooses of one's own free will. And the stimulus of talent will rise in your soul and stir restlessly until you gratify it.
—to Aleksei Suvorin, July 6, 1892 [LF]

★

Yes, I wrote to you once that you must be unconcerned when you write pathetic stories. And you did not understand me. You may weep and moan over your stories, you may suffer with your heroes, but I consider one must do this so that the reader does not notice it. The more objective, the stronger will be the effect.
—to Lidia Avilova, April 29, 1892 [LF]

*

Not long ago I had this experience: enters to see me a youth, a certain Shuf, with a thick writing-book, and tearfully asks me to read his poem, "The Bird," I think, and begs me to give him my opinion of it. He says that he read it to the professors, and that they were loud in their praises. I read it and heavenly cherubs! Terrible stuff! And altogether foolish. The author comes for a verdict; I conscientiously tell him my opinion and advise him not to write long poems. And what do you think happens next? Within a month the poem appears in the *European Herald!* I remain a fool, but that is not the pity. The pity is that after the professorial praise, and the *European Herald*, the young fellow, through human weakness, will from now on in every adverse criticism see an attack on his genius.
—to Aleksei Suvorin, October 18, 1892 [LF]

*

The story ought to begin with the phrase, "Somov, evidently, was agitated"; all that precedes, about the cloud that goes to sleep, and the sparrows, the field which stretches far away—all that is routine-like. You feel Nature, but you do not represent it as you feel it. Descriptions of Nature must above all be pictorial, so that the reader, reading and closing his eyes, can at once imagine the landscape depicted; but the aggregation of such images as the twilight, the somber light, the pool, the dampness, the silver poplars, the clouded horizon, the sparrows, the distant meadow—that is not a picture, for, however much I try, I can in no way imagine all this as a harmonious whole. In such stories as yours, descriptions of Nature are in place and do not detract from the effect only when they are à propos, when they help you communicate to the reader this or that mood, like music accompanying declamation. So, when taps are sounded, and the soldiers sing "Our Father"; when the commandant of the regiment returns at night, and then in the morning they lead a soldier to punishment, the landscape is altogether in place, and there you are a master. The flashing of the lightning is a strong effect; it would be sufficient to call attention to it once only, and not to emphasize it, for otherwise the impression is weakened and the reader's mood is destroyed.

The descriptions of objects are, as a rule, mechanical; "The shelves on the wall were filled with books." Why not say simply, "The shelves of books," or just "the bookshelves"? The volumes of Pushkin were "in disorder," the D. Library Edition is "scorched." And what of all that? You hold the reader's attention, and then tire it, since you detain him while you describe the disorder of a bookshelf or a damaged copy of *Hamlet*—this is the first weakness; secondly, all this is not simple; it is manneristic, and, as a method, old. These days only ladies write, "the program announced," "the face was framed in masses of dark hair." [. . .]

That is all. But all that is so little. As regards each of the points I have taken up, you can say: "That is a matter of taste"—and you will be right.

—to Aleksandr Zhirkevich, February 4, 1895 [LF]

★

You are right: the plot is a difficult and risky one to handle. I can tell you nothing definite; I can only advise you to put your story away in a strong-box for a year and then to read it. It will become clearer to you. I hesitate to judge it, for fear of falling into all sorts of errors.

The story is loosely put together: the preaching is much too obvious, and the figures are very vaguely sketched in. There are superfluous characters, e.g., the heroine's brother and mother. There are superfluous episodes, for instance, the events and conversations before the wedding, and everything else that concerns the marriage. But if these things are defects, they are not grave ones. I think that a more serious matter is that you were unable to do well in the development of the tale. In order to solve questions about degeneration, psychosis, etc., one should be scientifically informed as to these things.

As regards the importance of the disease. (Let us designate it [i.e., syphilis] modestly with the Latin letter S.). In the first place, S. is curable; secondly, when physicians find the patient suffering from some grave malady, such, for example, as spinal consumption (tabes), or cirrhosis of the liver, and if the ailment originated in S., they have good hopes of curing it, because S. can be cured. In degeneration and general nervousness, flabbiness, etc., S. is not the only cause that brings these results—there is a combination of many factors, as: vodka, tobacco, over-eating among the intellectual classes, distorted education, lack of physical exercise, conditions of city life, etc., etc. Besides, there are other diseases no less serious. For example, phthisis. So I think it is not for the artist to belabor people because they are diseased. Is it my fault that I have a headache? Is it Sidor's fault that he is infected with S., that he has less resistance to the disease than Tarass? Is it Akulka's guilt that her bones are wasted with consumption? There is no one to blame, and should the guilt be traceable, that is the affair of the health officers and not of artists.

The physicians behave abominably in your story. You make them forget their medical ethics and secrecy; and then they transport a gravely sick man, a paralytic, to the city! Wasn't the prey of the mysterious S. shaken to death in the tarantass? And the ladies in your story look upon S. as upon the nether pit. This is unnecessary. S. is no vice, no result of slack will-power, but an illness, and people infected with it are in need of tender and friendly treatment. It is shameful for a wife to flee from her sick husband, claiming that the disease is contagious, or that it is nasty. She may act in any way she pleases, but the author should be kindly to the fingertips. By the way, do you know that influenza too, brings serious effects to the organism?

Oh, there is not a thing in Nature that cannot result in harm and that cannot be carried on by inheritance. Even breathing is dangerous! Personally, I abide by the following rule: I present ailing people in those respects only that are characteristic and that are descriptive. I do not recognize "our nervous age," because human beings were nervous in all ages. The person who fears nervousness should become a sturgeon or a smelt; the sturgeon can commit only one act of foolishness and idiocy: it will land on a hook and then into a dish to be fried.

I should like you to undertake something cheerful, something bright-green, in picnic-style. Leave it to us physicians to portray cripples and black monks. I shall soon begin work on humorous stories, because my psychopathologic repertoire is almost exhausted.
—to Elena Shavrova, February 28, 1895 [LF]

★

I read your story with great pleasure. Your hand is acquiring firmness, and your style is improving. I like the whole story, except the ending, which appears to me to lack force. . . . But this is a matter of taste and not so important. If one is to talk about flaws one should not confine oneself to details. You have a defect and a very serious one. In my opinion it is this: you do not polish your things, and hence they seem frequently to be florid and overloaded. Your works lack the compactness that makes short things alive. There is skill in your stories; there is talent, literary sense, but very slight art. You put your characters together in the right way, but not plastically. You are either too lazy or you do not wish to slough off at one stroke all that is useless. To make a face from marble means to remove from the slab everything that is not the face. Do I make myself clear? Do you understand? There are two or three awkward expressions which I under-lined.
—to Elena Shavrova, November 17, 1895 [LF]

★

"When one has written a story I believe that one ought to strike out both the beginning and the end. That is where we novelists are most inclined to lie. And one must write shortly—as shortly as possible."
—in conversation with Ivan Bunin, late 1895 [SK-3]

★

There are a great many acting persons in your story; they are all interesting, but the effect is of over-crowding; they dissipate the attention of the reader in a thousand different directions, and, being heaped together in the limited space of your story, they fail to make a clear impression on the mind of the reader. There are two courses open to you: fewer characters, or write a novel. Decide. I think that the latter is the one you should choose. Fate itself seems to be in favor of a novel, as you are tempted, every time you write a story, by an array of characters, and you are unable to deny yourself the pleasure of crowding them into a mass.
—to Elena Shavrova, March 25, 1896 [LF]

★

Your story is a good, charming, clever thing. But the action is, as always, slow, and therefore the story seems in some places to drag. Imagine a great pond out of which flows a slender current of water; imagine on the surface of the pond a number of things: chips of wood, boards, empty barrels, leaves—all of them, because of the slow flowing of the water, seeming to be stationary and heaped up at the mouth of the stream. This is what occurs in your story—no movement, and a multitude of details that pile up into a great heap.
—to Elena Shavorova, November 20, 1896 [LF]

★

I read through your story "In the Hospital" in the clinic where I am now. I'm answering you lying down. The story is very good, starting from where I've marked it in red pencil. But the beginning is banal, unnecessary. You should continue, of course, provided that writing gives you pleasure—that's the first thing; the second is provided that you're still young and that you'll learn to punctuate in a correct and literary manner.

As for "A Fairy Tale," it seems to me that it's not a fairy tale but a collection of words like "gnomes," "fairy," "dew," "knights"—all these are fake diamonds, at least on our Russian soil, on which neither knights nor gnomes have ever set foot and where you'll scarcely ever find a person able to imagine a fairy that lunches on dew and sunbeams. Have done with that: you need to be a sincere artist, to write only what is or what, in your opinion, ought to be; you need to paint pictures.

I return to the first story. You oughtn't to write so much about yourself; when you write about yourself, you fall into exaggeration and risk ending with nothing to show. People either won't believe you or will react coldly to your gushing.
—to Rimma Vashchuk, March 27, 1897

★

Instead of being angry, reread my letter a little more attentively. It seems I clearly wrote that your story is *very good,* except the beginning, which gives the impression of a superfluous addition. Allowing you to write or not—that's not my business. I pointed out your youth to you because at thirty to forty years old it's too late to start; I pointed out the necessity of learning to place punctuation marks in a correct and literary manner because in artistic productions those marks often play the role of musical notes, and they can't be learned from a textbook—you need instinct and experience. Writing with pleasure doesn't mean playing a game, entertaining yourself. Experiencing pleasure from something means loving that thing.

Forgive me; it's hard for me to write. I'm still lying down.

Reread my letter once more and stop being angry. I was completely sincere, and now I'm writing to you again because I sincerely wish you success.
—to Rimma Vashchuk, March 28, 1897

★

I like your story, yet it's not your work; it's a translation from English. There's not a single Russian phrase in it—not one! I read it through with great pleasure, and I hasten to fulfill your wish—I am returning it to you, but only so that you will send me another story as fast as you can. I would like to track it from your beginning to the end you reach. Only please write more, because writing little leads nowhere. You have to hurry, you have to get your hand in quickly, so that by the age of thirty you will have defined yourself and won for yourself a certain position in the literary market.
—to Vladimir Argutinsky-Dolgorukov, April 28, 1897

★

"Why write about a man getting into a submarine and going to the North Pole to reconcile himself to the world, while his beloved at that moment throws herself with a hysterical shriek from the belfry? All this is untrue and does not happen in real life. One must write about simple things: how Peter Semionovich married Marie Ivanovna. That is all. And again, why those subtitles: a psychological study, genre, nouvelle? All these are mere pretense. Put as plain a title as possible—any that occurs to your mind—and nothing else. Also use as few brackets, italics, and hyphens as possible. They are mannerisms."
—in conversation with Aleksandr Kuprin, ca. 1900 [SK-3]

★

You ask what my opinion is about your stories. My opinion? Yours is an unmistakable talent, and a real, great talent. For instance, in your story "In the Steppe" it is expressed with extraordinary power, and I was even seized with envy that it was not I who wrote it. You are an artist, a wise man; you feel superbly, you are plastic; that is, when you describe a thing you see it and touch it with your hands. That is real art. There you have my opinion, and I am very glad to be able to express it to you. I am very glad, and if we came to know each other and talk for an hour or two you would be convinced how highly I value you, and what hopes I build on your talent.

Shall I speak now of defects? But that is not so easy. To speak of the defects of a talent is like speaking of the defects of a great tree growing in the orchard; the chief consideration is not the tree itself, but the taste of the man who is looking at the tree. Is not that so? I shall begin by saying that, in my opinion, you do not use sufficient restraint. You are like a spectator in the theater who expresses his rapture so unreservedly that he prevents both himself and others from listening. Particularly is this lack of restraint felt in the descriptions of Nature with which you interrupt your dialogues; when one reads those descriptions one wishes they were more compact, shorter, put, say, into two or three lines. The frequent mention of tenderness, whispering, velvetiness, and so on, gives to these descriptions a certain character of rhetoric and monotony—and they chill the reader, almost tire him. Lack of restraint is felt also in the descriptions of women ("Malva," "On the Rafts") and in the love. It is not vigor, nor breadth of touch, but plain unreserve. Then there is a frequent use of words unsuitable in stories of your type. "Accompaniment," "disc," "harmony"—such words mar.

You talk often about waves. In your descriptions of educated people there is a feeling of strain, and, as it were, wariness; that is not because you have not sufficiently observed educated people; you know them, but you do not know precisely from what side to approach them.

How old are you? I do not know you; I do not know from where you come nor who you are; but it seems to me that while you are still young you ought to leave Nizhni-Novgorod, and for a couple of years rub against literature and literary people; not in order to learn to crow like the rest, but in order finally to plunge headlong into literature and fall in love with her.

—Maxim Gorky, December 3, 1898 [SK-1]

*

Apparently you haven't quite understood me. I did not write to you of the crudeness but of the unfitness of foreign, not genuinely Russian, or rarely used words. With other writers such words as, for instance, "fatalistically," pass unnoticed, but your things are musical, harmonious, so that any crude little touch screams at the top of its voice. Of course, this is a matter of taste, and perhaps this is a sign of excessive irritability in me, or of the conservatism of a man who long ago adopted definite habits. In descriptions I can put up with "collegiate councillor" and "captain of the second rank," but "flirt" and "champion" (when they are used in descriptions) arouse my disgust.

Are you a self-taught man? In your stories you are a complete artist, and a cultured one in the truest sense. Least of all is crudeness characteristic of you; you are wise, and your feelings are subtle and elegant. Your best things are "In the Steppe" and "On the Rafts." [. . .] The only defect is lack of restraint, lack of grace. When a man spends the fewest number of movements on a certain definite action, that is grace. In your expenditure there is felt excess.

The descriptions of nature are artistic; you are a real landscape painter. But the frequent personification (anthropomorphism)—the sea breathes, the sky gazes, the steppe caresses, Nature whispers, speaks, mourns, and so on—such personifications make the descriptions somewhat monotonous, at times sugary, at times vague. Color and expressiveness in descriptions of Nature are attained only by simplicity, by such simple phrases as "the sun set," "it became dark," "it began to rain," and so on—and that simplicity is inherent in you to a high degree, rare to anyone among the novelists.

—to Maxim Gorky, January 3, 1899 [SK-1]

*

In order to suffer as few failures as possible in fiction writing or in order that those failures are not so sharply felt, you need to write more, 100 to 200 stories a year. There's the secret.

—to Aleksandr Chekhov, May 11, 1899 [BB]

*

"It is very difficult to describe the sea. Do you know the description that a schoolboy gave in an exercise? 'The sea is vast.' Only that. Wonderful, I think."
—in conversation with Ivan Bunin, 1899 [SK-3]

*

"You should not read your writing to other people before it is published. And it is most important never to take anyone's advice. If you have made a mess of it, let the blood be on your own head. Maupassant by his greatness has so raised the standard of writing that it is very hard to write; but we have to write, especially we Russians, and in writing one must be courageous. There are big dogs and little dogs, but the little dogs should not be disheartened by the existence of the big dogs. All must bark—and bark with the voice God gave them."
—in conversation with Ivan Bunin, ca. 1899 [SK-3]

*

More advice: when reading the proofs, cross out a host of concrete nouns and other words. You have so many such nouns that the reader's mind finds it a task to concentrate on them, and he soon grows tired. You understand it at once when I say, "The man sat on the grass"; you understand it because it is clear and makes no demands on the attention. On the other hand, it is not easily understood, and it is difficult for the mind, if I write, "A tall, narrow-chested, middle-sized man, with a red beard, sat on the green grass, already trampled by pedestrians, sat silently, shyly, and timidly looked about him." That is not immediately grasped by the mind, whereas good writing should be grasped at once—in a second. One thing more: you are by nature lyrical, the timbre of your soul is gentle. If you were a composer you would shun the writing of marches. To be rude, noisy, to hurt, to accuse violently, these things are not natural to your talent. So you will understand if I advise you not to be sparing when you read the proofs.
—to Maxim Gorky, September 3, 1899 [LF]

*

Art, and the stage in particular, is a field where one cannot walk without stumbling at times. There are many unsuccessful days and whole seasons of failure ahead of one; and there will be misunderstandings and great disappointments—one must be prepared for all this; one must expect this, and, in spite of everything, one must doggedly pursue one's path.
—to Olga Knipper, October 4, 1899 [LF]

*

Please do not publish a defense in the newspapers. That is not the business of belles-lettrists. To refute the little newspapers is the same as pulling the devil's tail, or trying to shout down a wicked old woman. And Samuels, especially the Odessa ones, will purposely provoke you in order to induce you to send them denials. Of all the writers whom I have known and know, only two wrote defenses: you and Potapenko. And they never ceased blaming Potapenko for his action, and he himself always regretted it. Even if they were to print that you are a forger, you must not deign to deny it; the only occasion when it is proper for us to print a defence is when we wish to shield another. Not for ourselves, but for another.
—to Aleksandr Chekhov, January 25, 1900 [LF]

*

Accusations, bitterness, anger, so-called "independence," i.e., attacks on the liberal and the new people, all that is not your role. The Lord gave you a good, tender heart—use it; write with a feeling pen, light-heartedly, without thought to aspersions cast upon you. [. . .] Be objective, regard everything with the eye of a good man, i.e., your own eye,—and sit down to write a novel about Russian life, not an arraignment of Russian life, but a joyous song of the Goldfinch[13] praising Russian life, and life in general, which comes to us but once, so that there is no sense in spending it to convict drones, old gossips, and committees. Dear Jean, treat nobly your gift and your own self, let your vessel sail the wide seas, but keep the helm in your hands. Pardon those who have injured you, stop thinking about yourself, and, I beg you, begin to write again.
—to Ivan Leont'ev (Shcheglov), February 2, 1900 [LF]

---

[13] Chekhov is making a pun on Shcheglov's name, which means goldfinch.

★

I have just been reading in the papers that you are writing a play. Write, write, write! It is necessary. Even should the play fail, don't let that discourage you. Failure will be soon forgotten, but a success, however slight, may be of vast service to the theater.
—to Maxim Gorky, September 8, 1900 [LF]

★

"The Three," by Gorky [. . .] made a favorable impression on me, but only as regards the style in which it is written. The girls are not true to life; such people do not exist; and there are no such conversations. Yet the work is pleasant to read. The portion that appeared in December I did not like; there was a sense of strain throughout all of it. Gorky should not labor with so serious a face (he does not write, he labors); it should all come easier, without effort and strain.
—to Vladimir Posse, March 3, 1901 [LF]

★

By all means, my good fellow, finish the play. You feel that it is not turning out as you should like, but don't trust your feeling, as it may deceive you. One usually dislikes a play while writing it, but afterwards it grows on one. Let others judge and make decisions
—to Maxim Gorky, September 24, 1901 [LF]

★

Five days have passed since I read your play ("The Petty Bourgeois"). I have not written to you till now because I could not get hold of the fourth act; I have kept waiting for it, and—I still have not got it. And so I have only read three acts, but that I think is enough to judge of the play. It is, as I expected, very good, written à la Gorky, original, very interesting; and to begin by talking of the defects, I have noticed only one, a defect incorrigible as red hair in a red-haired man—the conservatism of the form. You make new and original people sing new songs to an accompaniment that looks second-hand; you have four acts; the characters deliver edifying discourses; there is a feeling of alarm before long speeches; and so on, and so on. But all that is not important, and it is all, so to speak, drowned in the good points of the play. Perchikhin—how living! His daughter is enchanting, Tatyana and Piotr are also, and their mother is a splendid old woman. The central figure of the play, Nil, is vigorously drawn and extremely interesting!

In fact, the play takes hold of one from the first act. Only God preserve you from letting anyone act Perchikhin except Artyom, while Alekseiev-Stanislavsky must certainly play Nil. Those two figures will do just what's needed; Piotr—Meyerhold. Only Nil's part, a wonderful part, must be made two or three times as long. You ought to end the play with it, to make it the leading part. Only do not contrast him with Piotr and Tatyana, let him be by himself and them by themselves, all wonderful, splendid people independently of each other. When Nil tries to seem superior to Piotr and Tatyana, and says of himself that he is a fine fellow, the element so characteristic of our decent working man, the element of modesty, is lost. He boasts, he argues, but you know one can see what sort of man he is without that. Let him be merry, let him play pranks through the whole four acts, let him eat a great deal after his work—and that will be enough for him to conquer the audience with. Piotr, I repeat, is good. Most likely you don't even suspect how good he is. Tatyana, too, is a finished figure, only (a) she ought really to be a schoolmistress, ought to be teaching children, ought to come home from school, ought to be taken up with her pupils and exercise-books, and (b) it ought to be mentioned in the first or second act that she has attempted to poison herself; then, after that hint, the poisoning in the third act will not seem so startling and will be more in place. Telerev talks too much: such characters ought to be shown bit by bit between others, for in any case such people are everywhere merely incidental—both in life and on the stage. Make Elena dine with all the rest in the first act, let her sit and make jokes, or else there is very little of her, and she is not clear. Her avowal to Piotr is too abrupt, on the stage it would come out in too high relief. Make her a passionate woman, if not loving at least apt to fall in love . . . .

—to Maxim Gorky, October 22, 1901 [CG]

★

"You yourself aren't writing? . . . No! Well, that's good. But today's students, instead of studying, are either writing novels or making revolution . . . Yet," he objected to himself, "maybe that's actually better. As students, we drank beer and neglected our studies too. And now we've turned into such . . . old duffers." [. . .]

Another time, this is how it was [. . .]: "Before all else, my friends, there's no need to lie . . . What makes art so especially good is that there can be no lying in it . . . It's possible to lie in love, in politics, in medicine; it's possible to deceive people and the Lord God himself—such things have happened—but in art that can't be done."

He was silent a moment, as if waiting for objections from his unseen interlocutor, and, having waited in vain, continued: "Yet I'm often reproached—even Tolstoy reproached me for writing about trivialities, for having no positive heroes: revolutionaries, Alexander the Great, or even, like Leskov, simply honest police officers. . . . But where to take them from? I would be glad to!" He laughed mournfully: "Our life is provincial; the towns are unpaved, the villages impoverished, the people threadbare. . . . In our youth we all chirp exuberantly, like sparrows on manure, but by forty we're already old and starting to think about death. . . . What heroes are we?"
—in conversation with Aleksandr Tikhonov, June 23, 1902 [BB]

II.

THE SELF-CRITIC

I ALSO THANK you for the flattering invitation to continue collaborating. I am especially eager to collaborate with *Fragments*. The direction of your magazine, its appearance and the skill with which it is produced will attract to you, as it already has, others as well as myself.

I am all for little pieces, and if I were publishing a humor magazine, I would strike through all garrulities[14]. In the Moscow editorial offices, only I alone rebel against excessive length (which, however, doesn't prevent me from occasionally committing something of the sort . . . You shouldn't swim against the tide!), but at the same time I acknowledge that the framework of "thus far and no farther" causes me no small amount of woe. Coming to terms with these limitations can sometimes be very hard. For example . . . you don't accept articles of more than a hundred lines, for which there are reasons. . . . I have a theme. I sit down to write. The thought of "one hundred" and "no more" throws off my hand from the very first line. I compress as much as possible, I filter, I cross out—and sometimes (as my author's instinct tells me) to the detriment of both theme and (mainly) form. After compressing and filtering, I begin counting . . . When I've counted to 100—120—140 lines (I've never written more for *Fragments*), I get scared and . . . I don't send it. Just as soon as I start spilling over onto the fourth page of small-format postal paper, I begin having doubts, and I . . . don't send it. More often than not I have to hastily chew over the end and send what I wouldn't have wished to. . . . As a sample of my woes, I'm sending you the article "The Only Remedy" . . . I have compressed it, and I send it to you

---

[14] Продлинновенное is Chekhov's neologism. I thank Liv Bliss for this English neologism.

in the most compressed form, and all the same it seems to me that
it's damnably long for you, but meanwhile, it seems to me that were
I to write it twice as long, it would have twice the spice and sub-
stance. . . . There are some smaller things—and I fear for them. There
have been times when I might have sent them, but now I demur. . . .

Out of all this comes a request: grant me the right of up to 120
lines . . . I am certain that I will rarely make use of this right, but the
awareness that I have it will spare me from having my hand thrown
off.[15]
—to Nikolai Leikin, January 12, 1883 [BB]

★

You are not a newspaper man. He is a newspaper man who, smiling
into your eyes, sells your soul for thirty counterfeit silver coins, and
because you are better and bigger than himself he secretly seeks to destroy
you with another's hands—that is the newspaper man I wrote about.

But you, old man, are a puzzle, a smell, a gas, a nothing, a newspaper homunculus. I am a newspaper man because I write much, but
this is temporary. I shall not die one. If I am going to write, then
beyond doubt I shall do it from a distance, from a peep-hole. Don't
envy me, dear brother! Writing gives me nothing but twitches. The
hundred rubles I make a month sink into the belly and there's no
chance to change my shabby, indecent jacket into something less
ancient. I am paying on all sides and there remains nihil to me. More
than fifty goes on the family. There is no money to go with to
Voskressensk [for the summer holiday]. Nikolai, too, hasn't a damn.
At least I can comfort myself with the thought that there are no
creditors behind my back. I received from Leikin, for April, seventy
rubles, and here we are at the 19th and I haven't enough to take a cab.

Were I to live alone I could live like a rich man; but now by the
rivers of Babylon there we sat down and wept. Pastukhov took me
to supper to the Tiestov restaurant and promised six kopecks per
line. I could make in his paper not one but two hundred rubles a
month. But, you see for yourself, it is better to go without trousers,
with a bare posterior, and visit patients than to work for his paper.
The Alarm Clock I cannot stand, and if I were to agree to scribble for

---

[15] *Fragments* editor Leikin replied, "Assuming that you won't start indulging yourself
with too many excessively lengthy pieces, I give you my blessing for 120, 140,
even 150 [lines], provided you send something for every issue without fail."

it, it would be done with pain. The devil take them! If all journals
were as honest as *Fragments* I would ride about on horses. My stories
are not base, and, they say, they are better than others in form and
content; the Johnnies class me as a humorist of the first degree, as
one of the best, even the very best; my stories are read at literary
evenings; but it is better to treat loathsome diseases than to take
money for vile stories, for sneering at drunken shopkeepers [. . .].
The devil take them! Let us wait and see, and meanwhile let us go
in shabby coats. I shall plunge into medicine; there is salvation in it,
although I do not believe in myself as a medical man [. . .].
—to Aleksandr Chekhov, May 13, 1883 [SK-1]

*

This enclosure belongs to the lesser things. The notes are pale, and
the story unpolished and too petty. I have a better topic, and I could
write more, but fate is this time against me. I write in most hideous
circumstances.

Before me is my non–literary work mercilessly whipping my
conscience; the child of a relation who has come to stay with us
howls in the next room; in the other room my father is reading aloud
to mother "The Flaming Angel" . . . Someone has wound up the
music-box and I can hear "Fair Hélène." I long to run away to
the country, but it is one o'clock in the morning. It is hard to imagine a setting more abominable for a writing man. My bed is occupied
by a visitor [i.e. Chekhov's brother Aleksandr] who comes up to me
every now and then and starts a talk on medicine: "My little daughter must have a stomach ache—that is why she is crying."

I have the misfortune to be a medical man, and there is no one
who does not consider it necessary to chat with me on medicine, or,
when bored by medicine, to talk about literature. The setting is
incomparable. I rebuke myself for not having run off to the country,
where I could have a good sleep and write you a story. Above all,
medicine and literature would be left in peace. In September, the
weather permitting, I shall run away to Voskressensk. Your last story
has sent me into raptures.

The baby howls!! I give my word of honor never to have children.[16]
The French have few children, probably because they sit in their

---

[16] After his marriage to the actor Olga Knipper in 1901, his dearest wish was to have
a child with her. This unfortunately did not happen.

studies and write stories in *Amusant*. They say that someone wants
to make the French have more children—there is a theme for *Amusant*
and for *Fragments*—a caricature: "The state of France: enter a police
agent, who commands the parents to beget children."
—to Nikolai Leikin, August 21–24, 1883 [SK-1]

★

For the love of Allah! Do me a favor, boot out your depressed civil
servants! Surely you've picked up by now that this subject is long
out of date and has become a big yawn? And where in Asia have you
been rooting around to unearth the torments the poor little pen-
pushers in your stories suffer? For verily I say unto thee: they are
actively unpleasant to read! [. . .] It may be hard to resist the pressure to prune, but you have an easy remedy to hand: do it yourself,
pare it down to its limits, do your own rewriting. The more you
prune, the more often your work will get into print . . . But the most
important thing is: keep at it unstintingly, don't drop your guard for
an instant, rewrite five times, prune constantly.
—to Aleksandr Chekhov, January 4, 1886 [BB]

★

Having written and reread the story ["Poison"] I sent you yesterday,
I scratched myself behind the ear, raised my brows, and hemmed and
hawed—actions every author takes after having written something
long and boring . . . I began the story in the morning; the idea wasn't
bad and the beginning came out quite well too, but the misfortune
was that I was forced to write with intermissions. After the first
page, A. M. Dmitriev's wife came to ask for a medical certificate;
after the second, I received a telegram from Schechtel: *Unwell!* I had
to go off to attend to him . . . After the third page—lunch, and so
on. But writing with intermissions is just the same as having an
irregular pulse. [. . .]
    You asked me to speak candidly about your story ["Teachers'
Correspondence"]. In my opinion, the theme is very good and
gratifying; such themes suit *Fragments* very well. I also liked the
execution, though I hold the opinion that a presentation in the form
of letters is an outdated thing. It will suit if all the spice resides in the
letters themselves (showing, for example, how the district police
officer views things, presenting a series of love letters), but as a literary

form it does not suit in many respects. It encloses the author in a framework—that's the main thing. Had you written a story on this theme, that would have been better.
—to Nikolai Leikin, March 4, 1886 [BB]

*

Hitherto my attitude to my literary work has been frivolous, heedless, casual. I don't remember a *single* story over which I have spent more than twenty-four hours, and "The Huntsman," which you liked, I wrote in the bathing-shed! I wrote my stories as reporters write their notes about fires, mechanically, half-unconsciously, taking no thought of the reader or myself. . . . I wrote and did all I could not to waste upon the story the scenes and images dear to me which—God knows why—I have treasured and kept carefully hidden. [. . .]

  I give to literature my spare time, two or three hours a day and a bit of the night, that is, time which is of no use except for short things.
—to Dmitri Grigorovich, March 28, 1886 [CG]

*

My nom de plume, A. Chekhonte, is probably odd and fantastic. But it originated in the dawn of my misty youth; I have got used to it, and therefore I do not notice its oddness. I write comparatively little: not more than two or three short stories a week. I shall have time to work for *New Times*, but I am glad you do not make writing on fixed dates a condition of my contributing. Pressing work means hurry and a sense of burden, and these hamper one. Personally, pressing work is inconvenient to me for another reason: I am a doctor and practice medicine. I cannot guarantee that tomorrow I won't be dragged from my table for a whole day. There's the risk of not being ready in time, and of being constantly tardy.
—to Aleksei Suvorin, February 21, 1886 [SK-1]

*

My head has detached from my hand and refuses to create . . . The entire holidays, my brain has strained; I puffed and sniffed, a hundred times I sat down to write, but every time, from my "lively" pen, long things or sour ones or nauseated ones poured out, which doesn't go over for *Fragments*, and they were so bad, I decided not to send them to you so as not to embarrass my family name. [. . .]

I didn't send *New Times* a single story, to the *Gazette* some sort of 2 stories, and how on such dough I will live in February, God knows. . . . You are generally a skeptic, and you don't believe in human incapability, but I assure you by honest word, yesterday from morning to night, the whole day I toiled over a story for *Fragments*, lost the time, and lay down to sleep, not having written a page. . . . Laziness or a lack of desire is out of the discussion. . . . If you will be resentful and scold, you'll be wrong. I'm guilty, but I deserve indulgence!
—to Nikolai Leikin, January 12, 1887 [BB]

★

I'm sitting in an autumn coat trying to give birth to a Saturday Special [for the weekend edition of the *New Times* newspaper], but instead of thoughts, something thoroughly frostbitten is squeezing out of my head.
—to Nikolai Leikin, May 22, 1887 [BB]

★

Your letter is received; so as not to lie in bed and spit at the ceiling, I sit myself down at the table to answer.[17] I am ailing and depressed, like the son of a hen. The pen falls from my hand, and I do not write at all. I am expecting bankruptcy in the immediate future. If the play doesn't save me, then I am lost in the bloom of my years. The play may bring me 600 or 700 rubles, but not before the middle of November, and what will happen until that middle I know not. I *cannot* work, and everything I write turns out rubbish. My energy—*fuit!* [. . .]

I am scratching a Saturday feuilleton, but merely so-so, and on an unattractive theme to me. ["The Cattle-Dealers"] will turn out bad, but still I will send it.[18] [. . .]

---

[17] Chekhov may be referencing (and comparing himself to) Kovalev's idle servant Ivan in Nikolai Gogol's "The Nose," who does indeed spit at the ceiling while biding his time.

[18] "The Cattle-Dealers" ("Холодная кровь," literally "Cold Blood") was an especially successful story. It also won Chekhov recognition from the St. Petersburg Society for the Protection of Animals.

I wrote the [full-length] play *Ivanov* unexpectedly, after a talk with Korsh. I went to bed, thought out a theme, and wrote it. I spent a fortnight on it, or, rather, ten days, for there were days in the fortnight when I did not work or wrote something else. [. . .] It is a pity I cannot read the play to you. You are a light-minded man and have not seen much, but you are much fresher and keener-eared than all my Moscow praisers and accusers. Your absence is no small loss to me.
—to Aleksandr Chekhov, October 12, 1887 [SK-1]

★

My play, of the highest expectations—that it be simple!—has so taken me and tormented me that I lost the ability to orient the time, it knocked me off my legs, and probably I'll soon become a psycho. Writing it was not hard, but putting it on demands not only expenditures on cabs and time, but so much nervous work.
—to Nikolai Leikin, November 4, 1887 [BB]

★

Well, the first performance is over.[19] I will tell you all about it in detail. To begin with, Korsh promised me ten rehearsals, but gave me only four, of which only two could be called rehearsals, for the other two were tournaments in which *messieurs les artistes* exercised themselves in altercation and abuse. Davydov and Glama were the only two who knew their parts; the others trusted to the prompter and their own inner conviction.

Act One.—I am behind the stage in a small box that looks like a prison cell. My family is in a box of the benoire and is trembling. Contrary to my expectations, I am cool and am conscious of no agitation. The actors are nervous and excited, and cross themselves. The curtain goes up . . . the actor whose benefit night it is comes on. His uncertainty, the way that he forgets his part, and the wreath that is presented to him make the play unrecognizable to me from the first sentences. Kiselevsky, of whom I had great hopes, did not deliver a single phrase correctly—literally *not a single one*. He said things of his own composition. In spite of this and of the stage

---

[19] *Ivanov's* opening night was November 19, 1886.

manager's blunders, the first act was a great success. There were many calls.

Act Two.—A lot of people on the stage. Visitors. They don't know their parts, make mistakes, talk nonsense. Every word cuts me like a knife in my back. But—o Muse!—this act, too, was a success. There were calls for all the actors, and I was called before the curtain twice. Congratulations and success.

Act Three.—The acting is not bad. Enormous success. I had to come before the curtain three times, and as I did so Davydov was shaking my hand, and Glama, like Manilov, was pressing my other hand to her heart. The triumph of talent and virtue.

Act Four, Scene One.—It does not go badly. Calls before the curtain again. Then a long, wearisome interval. The audience, not used to leaving their seats and going to the refreshment bar between two scenes, murmur. The curtain goes up. Fine: through the arch one can see the supper table (the wedding). The band plays flourishes. The groomsmen come out: they are drunk, and so you see they think they must behave like clowns and cut capers. The horseplay and pot-house atmosphere reduce me to despair. Then Kiselevsky comes out: it is a poetical, moving passage, but my Kiselevsky does not know his part, is drunk as a cobbler, and a short poetical dialogue is transformed into something tedious and disgusting: the public is perplexed. At the end of the play the hero dies because he cannot get over the insult he has received. The audience, grown cold and tired, does not understand this death (the actors insisted on it; I have another version). There are calls for the actors and for me. During one of the calls I hear sounds of open hissing, drowned by the clapping and stamping.

On the whole I feel tired and annoyed. It was sickening though the play had considerable success. [. . .] Theater-goers say that they had never seen such a ferment in a theater, such universal clapping and hissing, nor heard such discussions among the audience as they saw and heard at my play. And it has never happened before at Korsh's that the author has been called after the second act. [. . .]
—to Aleksandr Chekhov, November 20, 1887 [CG]

*

In accordance with your friendly advice, I began writing a story for the *Northern Herald*. As a beginning, I undertook to describe the steppe, the people of the steppe, and all that I lived through there. It is a good theme, and it is pleasant to work on it, but unfortunately,

owing to lack of practice in writing long things, and from fear of crowding in too many details, I go to the opposite extreme: each page comes out compact, like a short story, the pictures multiply and huddle together, and, vying with one another for the reader's attention and interest, they spoil the single impression I wish to attain. As a result, one gets, not a picture in which all the details are emerged into a whole, like stars, in the heavens, but a mere summary, a dry inventory of impressions. A writer—you for instance—will understand me, but a reader will get bored and spit.
—to Vladimir Korolenko, January 9, 1888 [LF]

★

You give the announcement of my novel such hearty welcome that I am worried. . . . It is clear that you expect something really good— what a chance for disappointment! I quake and am in fear that my [novella] *Steppe* will not prove remarkable. I write slowly, as gourmands eat snipe, with sentimental gusto, with slow deliberation and pensiveness. Frankly speaking, I am forcing it out of myself, with panting and great exertion, but after all it does not satisfy me though in some places there are bits of "prose-poetry." I am not used to writing these long things. Short stories have spoiled me for them.
—to Aleksei Pleshcheev, January 23, 1888 [LF]

★

While writing [*Steppe*], I caught the odor of summer and the lure of the steppe. It would be fine to go there! For heaven's sake do not stand on ceremony and write me that the tale is poor and ordinary if that is your candid opinion. I want terribly to know the real truth.
—to Aleksei Pleshcheev, February 3, 1888 [LF]

★

I expended a lot of sap, energy and luminescence on my *Steppe*. I wrote intensely, strained, wrung it out of myself and exhausted myself most appallingly. Whether it succeeded or not, I don't know, but in any case it's my masterpiece. I can't do better, and your consolation that "sometimes things don't come off" (in case of failure) therefore can't console me. A debut, all that energy, the tension, a good plot and so on—your "sometimes" is scarcely applicable. If in the given

conditions I wrote wretchedly, that means I will write even worse under less propitious ones.
—to Aleksandr Lazarev-Gruzinsky, February 4, 1888 [BB]

★

I am in a hurry to start on something short, but I long for some large work. Oh, if you only knew what a plot for a novel I have in my mind! What wonderful women! What funerals! What marriages! If I had money I would rush off to the Crimea; I'd sit down under a cypress-tree, and I'd produce a novel inside of a month or two. I have already completed three signatures[20], can you imagine it! No, I exaggerate: if I had money to spend freely, then all the novels would fly to the wind.
—to Aleksei Pleshcheev, February 9, 1888 [LF]

★

You ask in the letter what I'm writing. After *Steppe*, I've done almost nothing. I began a gloomy story in the manner of Al'bov; I wrote around eight pages (not especially badly) and then tossed it aside until March. For something to do, I wrote a vacuous, Frenchified farce under the title of "The Bear," began a short story for *New Times*, and that's all. I wasted all of February. I paced back and forth or read my medical texts. There was so much sap and energy spent on *Steppe* that for a long time since I've been unable to take up anything serious.

Oh, if they find out at the *Northern Herald* that I'm writing farces they'll pronounce an anathema on me! But what can I do if my hands itch and want to perpetrate some sort of "folderol." No matter how I try to be serious, nothing comes of it, and my seriousness alternates with tawdriness. It must be in my stars. But seriously speaking, it's very possible that what's "in my stars" serves as a symptom of my never shaping up as a serious, dependable workman.
—to Yakov Polonsky, February 22, 1888 [BB]

★

---

[20] Forty-eight pages, with each signature (a piece of paper at a printer's shop that was destined to be cut and bound) comprising sixteen pages.

I'm publishing a new collection of my stories. In this collection there will be the story "Happiness," which I consider the best of all my stories. Be so kind as to allow me to dedicate it to you. With this, you will greatly oblige my muse. In the story, the steppe is described: the plains, the night, the white dawn in the east, a herd of sheep, and three human figures holding forth on happiness. I await your permission.

—to Yakov Polonsky, March 25, 1888 [BB]

★

Yesterday I gave the story I am writing for the *Northern Herald* to a girl to read. She read it and said, "Oh, how dull!" That's just it—it's really dull. I've tried every way of bringing it to life, have shortened it, polished, etc., but it remains dull in spite of all my efforts.

—to Vladimir Korolenko, April 9, 1888 [LF]

★

I would send a story now, but it serves no purpose to hurry. I am a coward and diffident; I am afraid to hurry, and altogether am afraid of being published. I keep on thinking that soon readers will get tired of me, and I shall become a contractor of ballast, like Yasinsky, Mamim, Bazhin, who, like myself, "held out great promise." That fear has a basis: I have been publishing for a long time, I have published five hundredweight of stories, but even yet I do not know in what is my strength and in what my weakness.

—to Aleksei Pleshcheev, April 9, 1888 [SK-1]

★

I am finishing the dullest story. I wished to include some philosophy, and the result is rosin and vinegar. I have just been reading over what I wrote, and I feel a sense of discomfort and nausea; it's disgusting. Well . . . Let's forget it! Whatever foolishness we write now—let the turkey-cock critics subtilize as much as they have a mind to—ten years from now we shall no longer be concerned about it all. Hence, good captain, go ahead without fear and doubt.

—to Ivan Leont'ev (Shcheglov), April 18, 1888 [LF]

★

You advise me not to hunt after two hares, and not to think of medical work. I do not know why one should not hunt two hares even in the literal sense. I feel more confident and more satisfied with myself when I reflect that I have two professions and not one. Medicine is my lawful wife and literature is my mistress. When I get tired of one I spend the night with the other. Though it's disorderly, it's not so dull, and besides, neither of them loses anything from my infidelity. If I did not have my medical work I doubt if I could have given my leisure and my spare thoughts to literature. There is no discipline in me.

—to Aleksei Suvorin, September 11, 1888 [LF]

*

I have one theme more: a young man of [Vsevolod] Garshin's spirit, uncommon, honest, and deeply sensitive, chances for the first time in his life to visit a brothel. As serious things are to be treated seriously, in this story everything will be called by its proper name. I may be able to write it so that it will produce, as I should like it to, a depressing effect; it may turn out quite good and suit the book; but can you, my dear fellow, guarantee that the censorship or the editors themselves will not scratch from it what I consider important? The book is an illustrated one and therefore subject to censorship. If you guarantee that not a single word will be struck out, I will get the story written in two evenings. But if you cannot—well, wait a week, and I'll give you my final answer; perhaps I'll find another theme. Honor to Shchedrin and Shcheglov, who write so much! Certainly, to work is better than not to work at all, and your reproach to the young writers is fully deserved. On the other hand, much writing does not suit every writer. Take myself, for instance. Last year I wrote *Steppe*, "Fires," one play, two farces, a mass of tiny stories, and began a novel . . . and—well? If that hundred poods of sand be washed the result will be (leaving out the fees) just five ounces of gold.

—to Aleksandr Pleshcheev, September 15, 1888 [SK-1]

*

I am afraid of those who look for a tendency between the lines, and who are determined to regard me either as a liberal or as a conservative. I am not a liberal, not a conservative, not a believer in gradual progress, not a monk, not an indifferentist. I should like to be a free

artist and nothing more, and I regret that God has not given me the power to be one. I hate lying and violence in all their forms, and am equally repelled by the secretaries of consistories and by Notovich and Gradovsky. Pharisaism, stupidity, and despotism reign not in merchants' houses and prisons alone. I see them in science, in literature, in the younger generation. That is why I have no preference either for gendarmes, or for butchers, or for scientists, or for writers, or for the younger generation. I regard the company and the label as a superstition. My holy of holies is the human body, health, intelligence, talent, inspiration, love, and the most absolute freedom—freedom from violence and lying, whatever forms they may take. This is the program I would follow if I were a great artist.
—to Aleksandr Pleshcheev, October 4, 1888 [LF]

★

Yes, my dear critic, you are right! The middle of my story ["The Name-Day Party"] is tedious, gray and monotonous. I wrote it lazily and carelessly. Having got accustomed to very short stories consisting of a beginning and an end only, I get weary and begin to I chew the cud when I am writing the middle. You are right also in hiding nothing, but expressing your suspicion straightforwardly. Am I not afraid to be regarded as a Liberal? This gives occasion for me to gaze inwards. It seems to me that I could rather be accused of gluttony, of drunkenness, of light-mindedness, of coldness, of anything than a desire to appear or not to appear. I have never hidden myself. If I am fond of you, or of Suvorin, or Mikhailovsky, I do not conceal it anywhere. If I feel sympathy for my heroine, Olga Mikhailovna, a radical and ex-student, I do not conceal it in my story, which seems sufficiently clear. Neither do I conceal my respect towards the Zemstvo, which I love, nor to the institution of trial by jury. True, an inclination to balance the pluses and minuses may be suspected in my story. But I do not balance conservatism as against liberalism, which to me do not represent the main point, but the falsity of the heroes as against their truth. Peter Dmitrich lies and plays the buffoon in court; he is ponderous and hopeless, but I cannot help showing that he is a lovable and sensitive man by nature. Olga Mikhailovna never stops lying, but it must not be disguised that to tell lies causes her pain.
—to Aleksei Pleshcheev, October 9, 1888 [SK-1]

★

I don't have any particular plans for the future. I want to write a novel, have got a marvelous plot. Sometimes I'm seized by a passionate desire to sit and get down to it, but I evidently lack the strength. I have begun and I'm afraid to continue. I have decided that I will write it without hurrying, only in my good hours, correcting and polishing. I'll spend several years on it. I don't have the spirit to write it all at one go, in one year; I fear I'm too weak. Besides, there's actually no need to hurry. I have a knack for not loving this year what was written in the last. It seems to me that next year I will be stronger than now, and this is why I'm not rushing now to risk making a decisive move. After all, if the novel comes out badly, it will all be over for me.

The thoughts, the women, the men, the pictures of nature that I have accumulated for the novel will remain whole and unscathed. I'm not frittering them away, I promise you that. My novel encompasses several families and a whole district with its woods, rivers, steamboats, railroad. In the center of the district are two main figures, a man and a woman, around whom the other chess pieces are grouped. I don't yet have a political, religious or philosophical worldview. I change it every month, so I have to limit myself to description only—how my heroes love, marry, give birth, die, and how they talk.

Until the novel's hour strikes, I will continue to write what I love—that is, short stories of sixteen to twenty-four printed pages or less. Stretching trifling plots onto a big canvas is boring albeit profitable. But it's a shame to tinker with big plots and squander images that are dear to me on pressing day-labor. I'll await a more convenient time.
—to Dmitri Grigorovich, October 9, 1888 [BB]

*

You write that the hero of "The Name-Day Party" is a character worth developing. Good Lord! I am not a senseless brute, you know; I understand that. I understand that I cut the throats of my characters and spoil them, and that I waste good material. . . . On my conscience, I would gladly have spent six months over the "Party"; I like taking things easy, and see no attraction in publishing in white-hot haste. I would willingly, with pleasure, with feeling, in a leisurely way, describe the whole of my hero, describe his state of mind while his wife was in labor, his trial, the unpleasant feeling he has after he is acquitted; I would describe the midwife and the doctors having tea in the middle of the night, I would describe the rain. . . . It would give me nothing but pleasure, because I like to take pains and dawdle. But what am I to do? I begin a story on September 10th with the thought that I must finish it by October 5th at the latest; if I don't I shall fail the editor and be left without money. I let myself go at the beginning and write with an easy mind; but by the time I get to the middle I begin to grow timid and to fear that my story will be too long: I have to remember that the *Northern Herald* has not much money, and that I am one of their expensive contributors. This is why the beginning of my stories is always very promising and looks as though I were starting on a novel, the middle is huddled and timid, and the end is, as in a short sketch, like fireworks. And so in planning a story one is bound to think first about its framework: from a crowd of leading or subordinate characters one selects one person only—wife or husband; one puts him on the canvas and paints him alone, making him prominent, while the others one scatters over the canvas like small coin, and the result is something like the vault of heaven: one big moon and a number of very small stars around it. But the moon is not a success, because it can only be understood if the stars too are intelligible, and the stars are not worked out. And so what I produce is not literature, but something like the patching of Trishka's coat. What am I to do? I don't know, I don't know. I must trust to time, which heals all things.

Speaking on my conscience again, I have not yet begun my literary work, though I have received a literary prize.[21] Subjects for five stories and two novels are languishing in my head. One of the novels was thought of long ago, and some of the characters have grown old without managing to get themselves written. In my head there is a whole army of people asking to be let out and waiting for the word of command. All that I have written so far is rubbish in comparison with what I should like to write and should write with rapture. It is all the same to me whether I write "The Name-Day Party" or "Lights," or a farce or a letter to a friend—it is all dull, spiritless, mechanical, and I get annoyed with critics who attach any importance to "Lights," for instance. I fancy that I deceive them with my work just as I deceive many people with my face, which looks serious or over-cheerful. I don't like being successful; the subjects which sit in my head are annoyed, jealous of what has already been

---

[21] The prestigious Pushkin Prize.

written. I am vexed that the rubbish has been done and the good things lie about in the lumber-room like old books. Of course, in thus lamenting I rather exaggerate, and much of what I say is only my fancy, but there is something of the truth in it, a good big part of it. What do I call good? The images which seem best to me, which I love and jealously guard lest I spend and spoil them for the sake of some "Party" written against time. . . . If my love is mistaken, I am wrong, but then it may not be mistaken! I am either a fool and a conceited fellow or I really am an organism capable of being a good writer. All that I now write displeases and bores me, but what sits in my head interests, excites, and moves me—from which I conclude that everybody does the wrong thing and I alone know the secret of doing the right one. Most likely all writers think that. But the devil himself would break his neck at these problems.

Money will not help me to decide what I am to do and how I am to act. An extra thousand rubles will not settle matters, and a hundred thousand is a castle in the air. Besides, when I have money—it may be because I am not accustomed to it, I don't know—I become extremely careless and idle; the sea seems only knee-deep to me then. . . . I need time and solitude.
—to Aleksei Suvorin, October 17, 1888 [LF]

*

I satisfied the women with "The Name-Day Party." Wherever I go, they praise it all around. Truly, it's not bad to be a doctor and understand what you're writing about. The ladies say the childbirth is described correctly.
—to Aleksei Suvorin, November 15, 1888 [BB]

*

I seem not to have brought off the play [a revision of *Ivanov*]. It is a pity, of course. Ivanov and Lvov present themselves to my imagination as living people. I tell you on my conscience, in all sincerity, these men were born in my head not out of sea-foam, not out of preconceived ideas, not out of "intellectuality," not accidentally. They are the result of my observation and study of life. They stand in my brain, and I feel that I have not falsified even by one centimeter nor sophisticated by a single jot. If on paper they have not come out clear and living, then the fault is not in them but in my inability to

express my thoughts. It shows that it is too early as yet for me to write plays.
—to Aleksei Suvorin, December 30, 1888 [SK-1]

★

It would give me great pleasure to read to the literary society a paper on how the idea of writing *Ivanov* occurred to me. I would make a public confession. I cherished a bold dream—to summarize all that had hitherto been written about whining and gloomy people, and with my *Ivanov* putting an end to such writings. It seemed to me that all Russian dramatists and novelists felt that they were compelled to depict low-spirited people, and that all of them wrote instinctively, without definite images or views on the matter. With my plot I have approximately hit the right spot, but the execution is no damned good. I ought to have waited! I am glad that I did not listen to Grigorovich two or three years ago, and write a novel. I can imagine what an amount of good material I should have spoiled had I listened to him. He says: "Talent and freshness will overcome anything." Talent and freshness can spoil a great deal—that is nearer the truth. Apart from abundance of material and talent, something else is needed no less important. Maturity is needed—that is one thing; secondly, the sense of personal freedom, and it was only recently that that sense began blazing up within me. Time was when I did not have it; lightmindedness, carelessness, and lack of respect for my work were successful substitutes.

What noble writers receive from nature gratis, the writers of the rank and file purchase at the cost of their youth. Do, please, write a story of how a young man, the son of a serf, who has been a shopboy, a chorister, pupil of a secondary school and a university graduate, who has been brought up to respect rank and to kiss the priest's hand, to bow to other people's ideas, to be thankful for each morsel of bread, who has been thrashed many a time, who has had to walk about tutoring without goloshes, who has fought, tormented animals, has been fond of dining at the house of well-to-do relations, and played the hypocrite both to God and man without any need but merely out of consciousness of his own insignificance—describe how that young man squeezes the slave out of himself drop by drop, and how, awakening one fine morning, he feels running in his veins no longer the blood of a slave but genuine human blood.
—to Aleksei Suvorin, January 7, 1889 [SK-1]

*

I'm writing my novel little by little. Whether anything will come of
it, I don't know, but when I'm writing it, it seems to me that I am
lying on new-mown hay in the garden, after a good lunch. Excellent
relaxation. Oh my, shoot me if I lose my mind and start meddling
with what doesn't concern me.
—to Aleksei Pleshcheev, January 15, 1889 [BB]

*

Where did you come up with the idea that I'm writing a lot? In the
whole of last year—in summer and winter, that is—I didn't even
finish five stories. I'm living on periodicals and plays. By contrast, I
ought to write more, but the *tolkastika*[22] is not there. Lermontov died
at twenty-eight but wrote more than you and me put together. Talent
is recognized not only by the quality but also by the quantity of work
it produces.
—to Piotr Sergeenko, March 6, 1889 [BB]

*

I intend to write a rather long tale. I have made a beginning already. I
shall not undertake a play very soon; I have no plots and no real
desire to write. In order to write for the theater one must love the
work, and without love nothing truly useful will result. Starting with
next season, I shall visit the theater regularly and educate myself in
stage ways.
—Vladimir Tikhonov, March 7, 1889 [LF]

*

Yesterday I finished and made a clean copy of a story, but it's my
novel which occupies me at present. Oh, what a novel! If it weren't
for the thrice-be-damned conditions of the censorship, I would
have promised it to you by November. There's nothing in the novel
promoting revolution, but the censor will tamper with it all the same.
Half of the characters say: "I don't believe in God." There's one
father whose son gets life at hard labor for armed resistance; there's

---

[22] Chekhov's term for the self-motivation to write (footnote by Liv Bliss).

a policeman ashamed of his uniform, a despised leader, and so on. Rich material for the [censor's] red pencil. [. . .]

Now is the very best time to embark on a big affair (a novel, of course, not a romance). If I don't write it now, when will I write it? That's my reasoning, though I'm almost sure that in two to three weeks, the novel will sicken me, and I'll again lay it aside.

I have the plot for a short story. I'll try to finish this story for the May or June issue. But if it were possible to wait until July or August, then my novel would give you many thanks.

Shed the censorship, for the creator's sake! Though up to now it has deleted almost nothing, all the same I'm afraid of it and don't love it. For thick magazines and newspapers, the censorship ought not to exist, not even in Turkey.
—to Anna Evreinova, March 10, 1889 [BB]

★

I am writing a novel! I keep writing and writing and I don't see the end of it all. I started at the beginning once more, carefully correcting and abridging everything that had already been written. I have already sketched nine figures, clearly and amply. What a plot! I call the novel simply, "Stories from the Life of My Friends." I am writing it in the form of separate, complete stories, closely connected by the common plot, idea, and characters. Each separate story has its own title. Do not imagine that the novel will consist of independent pieces. No, it is a regular novel, an entity, in which each figure is organically necessary. Grigorovich, to whom you handed the first chapter, expressed doubts about the fact that in it there is a student who is doomed to die, and therefore will not last through the entire novel, i.e., he is superfluous. But this student is just one nail driven into the heel of a large boot. He is a detail, incidental. It will not be easy to master the technique. The work is still weak in this respect, and I fear that there are many mistakes. It will be long-winded, I fear, and will contain foolish things. But I try to avoid dealing with unfaithful wives, suicides, fights, virtuous peasants, devoted servants, clever old women, provincial wits, red-nosed captains, and "new" people, though in some places I fall foul of this last species.[23]
—to Aleksei Suvorin, March 11, 1889 [LF]

---

[23] Chekhov never finished this novel.

★

I am practicing medicine. The center of that unlucky, very distasteful and tiresome practice is the sick-bed of my artist brother, who is down with typhus. I am a faint-hearted man; I cannot look straight in the face of circumstances, and you will believe me when I tell you that I am literally unable to work. These last three weeks I have not written a single line; I have forgotten all my subjects, and can think of nothing that might be of interest to you. I am boring beyond words.

My novel made considerable headway, but ran aground waiting for a tide. I am dedicating it to you—I have already written you about that. The lives of good people, their faces, deeds, words, thoughts and hopes are the foundation of this novel; my purpose is to kill two hares at once: to paint life faithfully and to show by the way how far that life deviates from the norm. The norm is unknown to me, as it is to any one of us.

We all know what a dishonest act is, but what honor is we do not know. I shall keep to the framework nearest to my heart, which has already been tried by men stronger and wiser than I. The framework is the absolute freedom of man, freedom from violence, from prejudices, ignorance, the devil, freedom from passions, etc.

I am sick of criticism. When I read a review I am seized with this horror: Are there really so few intelligent people on this earth that there is no one to write criticism? Monstrously stupid, petty and personal even to vulgarity it all is. It begins to appear to me that the reason we have no criticism is because it is not needed, just as fiction (modern, of course) is not needed.

—to Aleksei Pleshcheev, April 9, 1889 [SK-1]

★

I'm not working but reading or pacing back and forth. Yet I don't regret having the time to read. Reading is more cheerful than writing. I think that if I could live another forty years, and if in all those forty years I could read, read and read some more and learn to write with talent—concisely, that is—then in forty years' time I would fire such a big cannon at all of you that the heavens would shake. Now I'm as much a Lilliputian as everyone else.

—to Aleksei Suvorin, April 18, 1889 [BB]

★

You say I have grown lazy. That does not mean that I am now lazier than I used to be. I work nowadays as much as I did three or five years ago. To work, and to look as though I were working constantly from nine in the morning till dinner, and after the evening meal until bed-time, has become a habit with me, and in that respect I am exactly like a government clerk. And if my work does not result in two novels a month or in an income of ten thousand rubles, it is not my laziness that is to blame, but my inborn psychological peculiarities. I do not care enough for money to make a success of medicine, and for literature I have not enough passion, and therefore not enough talent. The fire burns in me slowly and evenly, without sudden spluttering and flaring up. And this is why I cannot cover reams of paper each night, or be so carried away by my work that it keeps me from bed when I am sleepy; this is why I commit no particular follies, or accomplish anything very wise.

I am afraid that in this respect I resemble Goncharov, whom I don't like, who is ten heads taller than I am in talent. I have not enough passion; add to that this sort of lunacy for the last two years I have for no reason at all ceased to care about seeing my work in print, have become indifferent to reviews, to literary conversations, to gossip, to success and failure, to good pay—in short, I have gone downright silly. There is a sort of stagnation in my soul. I explain it by the stagnation in my personal life. I am not disappointed, I am not tired, I am not depressed, but simply, everything has suddenly become less interesting. I must do something to rouse myself.
—to Aleksei Suvorin, May 4, 1889 [LF]

*

Shcheglov is not my rival. I do not know his play, but I have a presentiment that in my first two acts I have done ten times more than he has in all his five acts. His play may have a greater success than mine, but of such competition I am not afraid. I tell you this in order to show you how satisfied I am with my work. The play turned out tedious, like mosaic work, yet it gives me the impression of a real work. Positively new characters come through; there is not a single footman, a single comic relief character, a single widow, in the whole play. Altogether there are eight characters, and of those only three are episodical. Generally, I tried to avoid the superfluous, and I think I have managed it. In a word, there is no gainsaying I am a clever boy. If the censorship doesn't give it a thump in the neck, you

will in the autumn taste a delight beyond anything you could experience even if you stood on the top of the Eiffel Tower and looked down on Paris.
—to Aleksei Suvorin, May 14, 1889 [SK-1]

★

I replied to [the editor] Anna Mikhailovna's telegram with a letter, imploring her to wait (for my story) till the November number. She replied: "Let it be as you please. We will postpone." You will understand all the value and charm of that answer, if you can picture Mr. Chekhov writing, sweating, correcting, and seeing that for all the revolutionary disturbances and terrors the story is undergoing under his pen, it gets not the least bit better. I am not writing but occupied in perturbations. In such a mood, you must agree, it is not quite convenient to hurry into print. In my story there are not two moods, but fifteen. It is quite possible you will call the story patchwork. It is really patched. But I flatter myself with the hope that you will find in it two or three new faces, interesting to every intelligent reader; and also you will notice one or two new situations. I further flatter myself with the hope that my rag will produce some stir and abuse in the enemy camp. And without that abuse one can't manage, for in our times, the days of telegraphs, of Mme. Goriev's theater and of telephones, abuse is advertisement's own sister. [. . .]

Though I lack what Korolenko has, I possess something else. In my past I have a multitude of mistakes which Korolenko has not, and where there are mistakes there is experience. Besides, my battlefield is wide and my choice richer; except novels, verses and the laying of information, I have tried everything. I have written stories, sketches, farces, leading articles, humorous stuff, and all sorts of nonsense, including "Mosquitoes" and "Flies" for *The Dragonfly*. If a long tale failed me I could take up short stories; if the latter were bad, I could turn to farce, and so on without end to my very torpid death. So, with all my desire to look at myself and Korolenko with the eye of a pessimist and get in the dumps, I cannot get despondent, since up to now I have not seen the data for or against it. Let us wait for another five years; then it will be clear.
—to Aleksei Pleshcheev, September 14, 1889 [SK-1]

★

Story-writing as well as the theater has its conventions. My instinct tells me that in the finale of a novel or a story I must artificially concentrate in the reader the impression of the whole, and for this purpose mention—if only lightly, in a flash—characters of whom I have spoken before. It may be I am mistaken.
—to Aleksei Pleshcheev, September 30, 1889 [SK-1]

★

If you are given coffee do not look in it for beer. If I present you with the thoughts of the professor, believe me and don't look in them for Chekhov's thoughts. Thanks. In the whole story ["A Tedious Story"] there is only one idea which I share and which sits in the head of the professor's son-in-law, the rogue Gnekker, and it is, "The old fellow is gone crazy!" But all the rest is imagined . . . .
—to Aleksei Suvorin, October 17, 1889 [SK-1]

★

You say that writers are God's elect. I will not contradict you. Shcheglov calls me the Potemkin of literature, and so it is not for me to speak of the thorny path, of disappointments, and so on. I do not know whether I have ever suffered more than shoemakers, mathematicians, or railway guards do; I do not know who speaks through my lips—God or someone worse.
—to Aleksei Suvorin, December 1889[24] [LF]

★

A year after his brother Nikolai died of tuberculosis—the disease that eventually killed Chekhov—Chekhov decided to travel across the entirety of Russia, through Siberia. He conducted medical and sociological surveys on the prison island, Sakhalin, on Russia's Pacific coast.

About Sakhalin we are both mistaken, but you probably more than I. I am going in the full conviction that my visit will furnish no contribution of value either to literature or science: I have neither the knowledge, nor the time, nor the ambition for that. I have neither the plans of

---

[24] The first sheet of the letter containing the exact date in December has disappeared.

Humboldt nor of a Kennan.[25] I want to write some 100 to 200 pages[26], and so do something, however little, for medical science, which, as you are aware, I have neglected shockingly. Possibly I shall not succeed in writing anything, but still the expedition does not lose its charm for me: reading, looking about me, and listening, I shall learn a great deal and gain experience. I have not yet travelled, but thanks to the books which I have been compelled to read, I have learned a great deal which anyone ought to be flogged for not knowing, and which I was so ignorant as not to have known before. Moreover, I imagine the journey will be six months of incessant hard work, physical and mental, and that is essential for me, for I am a Little Russian and have already begun to be lazy. I must take myself in hand. My expedition may be nonsense, obstinacy, a craze, but think a moment and tell me what I am losing if I go. Time? Money? Shall I suffer hardships? My time is worth nothing; money I never have anyway; as for hardships, I shall travel with horses, twenty-five to thirty days, not more, all the rest of the time I shall be sitting on the deck of a steamer or in a room, and shall be continually bombarding you with letters.

Suppose the expedition gives me nothing, yet surely there will be two or three days out of the whole journey which I shall remember all my life with ecstasy or bitterness, etc., etc. . . . So that's how it is, sir. [. . .] No, I assure you that Sakhalin is of use and of interest to us, and the only thing to regret is that I am going there, and not someone else who knows more about it and would be more able to rouse public interest. Nothing much will come of my going there.[27]
—to Aleksei Suvorin, March 9, 1890 [CG]

★

Incited by hope of gain, but partly also by inspiration, I have written a story which I am sending together with this letter. Only, my dear fellow, send me the proof-sheets, for it is written with a blacking-brush, and needs after-touches. Much curtailing is necessary, and some revision; I would revise it now, but my head is set to the tune of Sakhalin, and as regards everything that has to do with elegant

---

[25] The German explorer Alexander von Humboldt and the American journalist George Kennan had both written books about their travels across Siberia.

[26] Chekhov published *Sakhalin Island*, 500 pages' worth, in 1895.

[27] Chekhov's *Sakhalin Island* would in fact bring public attention and remedies to the deplorable conditions on Sakhalin.

literature, I am not in a position to distinguish bad from worse. I shall have to wait and read it in proof.
—to Aleksei Suvorin, March 15, 1890 [LF]

*

When I set off I promised to send you notes of my journey after Tomsk, since the road between Tyumen and Tomsk has been described a thousand times already. But in your telegram you have expressed the desire to get my impressions of Siberia as quickly as possible, and have even had the cruelty, sir, to reproach me with lapse of memory, as though I had forgotten you. It was absolutely impossible to write on the road. I kept a brief diary in pencil and can offer you now only what is written in that diary. To avoid writing at great length and getting mixed up, I divided all my impressions into chapters. I am sending you six chapters. They are written *for you personally*. I wrote for you only, and so have not been afraid of being too subjective, and have not been afraid of there being more of Chekhov's feelings and thoughts of Siberia in them. If you find some lines interesting and worth printing, give them a profitable publicity, signing them with my name and printing them in separate chapters, a tablespoonful once an hour. The general title can be *From Siberia*, then *From Trans-Baikalia*, then *From the Amur*, and so on.

You shall have another helping from Irkutsk, for which I am starting tomorrow. I shall not be less than ten days on the journey—the road is bad. I shall send you a few chapters again, and shall send them whether you intend to print them or not. Read them and when you are tired of them telegraph to me "Shut up!" [. . .]

If my letters are short, careless, or dry, don't be cross, for one cannot always be oneself on a journey and write as one wants to. The ink is bad, and there is always a hair or a splodge on one's pen.
—to Aleksei Suvorin, May 20, 1890 [CG]

*

Chekhov had finished his exhausting fieldwork on Sakhalin and was sailing home through the Pacific and Indian oceans on the steamer Baikal.

I have seen *everything*, so that the question is not now *what* I have seen, but how I have seen it. I don't know what will come of it, but I have done a good deal. I have got enough material for three dissertations. I got up every morning at five o'clock and went to bed late; and all day long was on the strain from the thought that there was still so much I hadn't done; and now that I have done with the convict system, I have the feeling that I have seen everything but have not noticed the elephants.

By the way, I had the patience to make a census of the whole Sakhalin population. I made the round of all the settlements, went into every hut and talked to everyone; I made use of the card system in making the census, and I have already registered about ten thousand convicts and settlers. In other words, there is not in Sakhalin one convict or settler who has not talked with me. I was particularly successful with the census of the children, on which I am building great hopes.
—to Aleksei Suvorin, September 11, 1890 [CG]

*

In the latest issue of *The News of Foreign Literature* there is a story by Ouida, translated from the English by our Mikhail [Chekhov's youngest brother], the customs official. Why don't I know foreign languages? It seems to me that I could translate literary things with good effect. When I read translations by another hand, I keep altering and transposing the words in my mind, and I experience a sensation of something light, ethereal, like lacework.

On Mondays, Tuesdays, and Wednesdays I write my Sakhalin book, on the other days, except Sunday, my novel, and on Sundays, short stories.
—to Aleksei Suvorin, May 10, 1891 [LF]

*

All day yesterday I had my troubles with the Sakhalin book. It is difficult to write about such things, but after all, in the end I got the devil by the tail. I rendered the climate so vividly that you will feel the cold when reading. But how unpleasant to have to give statistics!
—to Aleksei Suvorin, May 18, 1891 [LF]

*

I shall finish my story [*The Duel*] tomorrow or the day after, but not today, as towards the end it has tired me devilishly. Owing to the haste of the work, I have spent a pound of nerves upon it. Its composition is a bit complicated. I got into tangles and often tore up what I had written. For days at a time I was dissatisfied with the work—that is the reason why I have not finished it till now. How horrible! I shall have to copy it out. It is impossible to leave it, for it is in a devil of a muddle. Lord! if the public likes my works as little as I do those of others I am now reading, what an ass I must be. There is something asinine in our profession.

It is impossible to improve my circumstances—that is, to make them different or better. There are the ailing who can be cured only by the sole, simple, and short method, namely: "Rise, take thy staff and walk." But I lack the power to take up my staff and walk; therefore, there is nothing to talk about.

—to Aleksei Suvorin, August 6, 1891 [SK-1]

★

At last I have finished my long, tiresome story [*The Duel*], and am sending it to you by registered post to Feodosia. Read it. It is too long for the newspaper, and because of its contents it would not do to break it up into parts. Well, do as you like. [. . .]

There are more than four signatures of print in the story. It is awful. I became exhausted and dragged the end, like a train of wagons on a muddy autumn night: slowly and with many halts. That is why I was late.

—to Aleksei Suvorin, August 18, 1891 [SK-1]

★

Sakhalin is going ahead. There are times when I long to sit at it for three or five years and work at it furiously; but there are others, in moments of doubt, when I could just take and cast it out. By Jove! it would be fine to give three years to it! I shall write a great deal of rubbish, since I am not a specialist, but verily I shall write something good too. And *Sakhalin* is good for this reason: it should live a hundred years after me as a literary source and guide to all who are at work, or are interested, in the penitentiary system.

—to Aleksei Suvorin, August 30, 1891 [LF]

★

I am leading the life of a privileged vegetable which is constantly poisoned by the thought that it must write, eternally write. I am writing a story. Before publishing it, I should like to send it to you for correction—for your opinion is golden to me—but it is necessary to hurry, as there is no money.

—to Aleksei Suvorin, March 31, 1892 [LF]

★

My soul has wilted from the consciousness that I am working for money and that money is the center of my activity. This gnawing feeling, added to a sense of justice, makes my authorship a contempt- ible pursuit in my eyes; I do not respect what I write, I am apathetic and bored with myself, and I am glad I have my medicine, which, at any rate, I don't practice for the sake of money. I ought to have a bath in sulfuric acid, flay off my skin, and then grow a new hide.

—to Aleksei Suvorin, June 16, 1892 [SK-1]

★

I have an interesting subject for a comedy, but I have not as yet thought of an ending. Whoever will invent new endings for plays will open a new era. The wretched endings won't come! The hero either marries or shoots himself, there is no other way out. My future comedy is called "The Cigar-Case."[28] I shall not go on with it until I think of an ending as good as the beginning. And when I do get hold of the ending, I shall write the thing in two weeks.

—to Aleksei Suvorin, June 4, 1892 [LF]

★

I worked hard on this book but felt for a long time that I was on the wrong path until I spotted the trouble. It was the illusion that my Sakhalin book was intended to teach certain things, and yet that I was holding something back, that I was not letting myself go. But no sooner had I begun to recount the funny things I remembered, and the pigs I saw in Sakhalin, than the work progressed beautifully. Still, there is very little humor in the book.

—to Aleksei Suvorin, July 28, 1893 [LF]

---

[28] The future never arrived for "The Cigar-Case."

*

I am really going to write small things. My dream is to build my own house in the woods that I possess, to plant roses, to give orders that I receive no one, and to write tiny stories. I know a wonderful spot for the house.
—to Aleksei Suvorin, August 24, 1893 [SK-1]

*

Not for one moment does the thought leave me that I must, that I am obliged to write. To write, and write, and write. I am of the opinion that inner happiness is impossible without idleness. My ideal: to be idle and love a fat girl. For me the greatest delight is to walk, or to sit and do nothing; my favorite occupation, to collect what is not needed (papers, bits of straw, etc.), and to do useless things. Meanwhile I am a litterateur, and must write, even here in Yalta. Dear Lika, when you become a big girl, and are given a huge allowance, then be so good as to marry me and feed me at your cost, so that I may do nothing. And if you are really going to die, then let Varya Eberlai do this for me; I like her, as you know. I am so shattered by the constant thought of inexorable, implacable work, that it is already a week since I have been tortured by ceaseless palpitations of the heart.
—to Lidia Mizinova, March 27, 1894 [LF]

*

The censor struck out of my story the lines which refer to religion. *Russian Thought* sends its contributions to be passed by preliminary censorship. This robs one of any desire to write freely. I write, but feel a bone in my throat all the time.
—to Aleksei Suvorin, January 19, 1895 [SK-1]

*

[. . .] imagine it!—I am writing a play [*The Seagull*] which is not likely to be finished before the end of November. I am writing it not without pleasure, although I am abusing terribly the conventions of the stage. It is a comedy with three female parts, six male parts, four

acts, a landscape (a view of a lake), much talk about literature, little action, and five tons of love.
—to Aleksei Suvorin, October 21, 1895 [SK-1]

★

The play [*The Seagull*] has fallen flat, and come down with a crash. There was an oppressive strained feeling of disgrace and bewilderment in the theater. The actors played more than stupidly. The moral of it is, one ought not to write plays.
—to Mikhail Chekhov, October 18, 1896 [LF]

★

You cannot imagine how your letter rejoiced me. I saw from the front only the first two acts of my play. Afterwards I sat behind the scenes and felt the whole time that *The Seagull* was a failure. After the performance that night and next day, I was assured that I had hatched out nothing but idiots, that my play was clumsy from the stage point of view, that it was not clever, that it was unintelligible, even senseless, and so on and so on. You can imagine my position—it was a collapse such as I had never dreamed of! I felt ashamed and vexed, and I went away from Petersburg full of doubts of all sorts. I thought that if I had written and put on the stage a play so obviously brimming over with monstrous defects, I had lost all instinct and that, therefore, my machinery must have gone wrong for good.

After I had reached home, they wrote to me from Petersburg that the second and third performances were a success; several letters, some signed, some anonymous, came, praising the play and abusing the critics. I read them with pleasure, but still I felt vexed and ashamed, and the idea forced itself upon me that if kind-hearted people thought it was necessary to comfort me, it meant that I was in a bad way. But your letter has acted upon me in a most definite way. I have known you a long time, I have a deep respect for you, and I believe in you more than in all the critics taken together—you felt that when you wrote your letter, and that is why it is so excellent and convincing. My mind is at rest now, and I can think of the play and the performance without loathing.
—to Anatoli Koni, November 11, 1896 [LF]

★

You complain that my heroes are gloomy—alas! that's not my fault. This happens apart from my will, and when I write it does not seem to me that I am writing gloomily; in any case, as I work I am always in excellent spirits. It has been observed that gloomy, melancholy people always write cheerfully, while those who enjoy life put their depression into their writings. And I am a man who enjoys life; the first thirty years of my life I have lived, as they say, in pleasure and content.
—to Lidia Avilova, October 6, 1897 [LF]

★

Many themes are rusting in my brain. I long to write, but to write away from home is a real labor, like sewing with someone else's sewing machine.
—to Maria Chekhova, December 14, 1897 [SK-1]

★

You have expressed a desire in one of your letters that I should send you an international story, taking for my subject something from the life here. Such a story I could write only in Russia, from memory. I can write only from memory, and have never written directly from nature. I have to let the subject filter through my memory so that only what is important or typical is left, as in a filter.
—to Fiodor Batyushkov, December 15, 1897 [SK-1]

★

I am disgusted with writing and I do not know what to do. I'd take up medicine with pleasure; I would look for a post, but I haven't the physical flexibility. When I write, or think about writing, I experience an aversion—as if I were eating sour-cabbage soup from which a roach had just been removed—forgive the comparison. It is not writing itself toward which I feel this aversion—it is really toward the literary "entourage" which one cannot escape, and which one always carries along as the earth carries its atmosphere.
—to Lidia Avilova, July 25, 1898 [LF]

*

"Before, I wrote the way a bird sings. *I sit down and write. I don't think about how or about what.* It went all by itself. I could write whenever it pleased me. Writing a sketch, a story, a skit, it didn't cost me any trouble. Like a little lamb or colt let loose into the open, I hopped, cavorted, kicked, wagged my tail, shook my head funnily. It was fun to me and from the outside it must have appeared very funny. I myself sometimes take up the old stories, read them and laugh. I think, 'I wrote like that.'"
—in conversation with Grigoriy Petrov, ca. 1900 [BB]

*

"If I leave a story for a long time, I cannot make myself finish it afterwards. I have to start it again."
—in conversation with Aleksandr Kuprin, ca. 1900 [SK-3]

*

I am receiving from Moscow letters from the performers of *Uncle Vanya*. They are heartbroken after having been so agitated, rehearsed so much, been so nervous. They expected a furor, and after all there is only an ordinary success, and this irritates the young artists. I have worked for twenty-one years, and I know that an average success is, for the writer and the actor, the best kind of success. After a triumph a reaction always sets in, expressing itself in heightened expectation, followed eventually by certain disappointment and cooling,—the reaction explaining it physiologically.
—to Piotr Kurkin, November 2, 1901 [LF]

*

About the play I will say this: (1) It is true my play is planned, and that I already have a title for it (*The Cherry Orchard*—but it is still a secret), and I shall settle down to write it not later, probably, than the end of February, if, of course, I am well; (2) the central character in the play is an old woman—to the great regret of the author; and (3) if I let the Art Theater have the play, then, according to its conditions and rules, it has the exclusive disposal of the play both for Moscow as well as for Petersburg—and there is no getting out of it.

If the Art Theater does not go to Petersburg in 1904 (which is quite likely; are they going this year?), there can be no doubt that, if the play suits you, I will let you have it with pleasure. Or, perhaps this will do. Shall I write a play *for you*? Not for this or that theater, but for you. This has long, long been my dream. Well, as God wills it. If I had my former health I would not be talking about it, but would simply sit down to write the play at once.

[. . .] You are a real actress, and that is the same as being a good sailor: in whatever ship, government or private, he may sail, everywhere and in all circumstances he remains a good sailor.
—to Vera Kommissarzhevskaya, January 27, 1903 [SK-1]

★

I should so very much like to see the rehearsals. I am afraid lest Anya's tone is too tearful (for some reason you find her similar to Irina). I fear that a young actress might not be given the part. Anya doesn't once shed tears; nowhere does she speak in a weeping tone; in Act II, though she has tears in her eyes, her tone is cheerful and lively. Why do you say in your telegram that there are many tearful people in the play? Where are they? Varya is the only one, and that is because she is a cry-baby by nature, and her tears should not provoke depression in the spectator. Frequently one meets the remark "through tears," but that merely denotes the mood of the character, not tears.
—to Vladimir Nemirovich-Danchenko, October 23, 1903 [SK-1]

★

I made Chekhov's acquaintance during the production of The Cherry Orchard, *at a rehearsal of Act II. I acted the part of Lopakhin. When he noticed that in Act II the actors began driving off the mosquitoes, he said:* "In the next play I shall make a character say: 'What a wonderful place, there is not a single mosquito here!'"
—in conversation with Leonid Leonidov, 1904 [SK-2]

III.

LITERARY QUESTIONS

ONE MEETS EVERY critical article with a silent bow even if it is abusive and unjust—such is the literary etiquette. It is not the thing to answer, and all who do answer are justly blamed for excessive vanity. But since your criticism has the nature of "an evening conversation [. . .]," and as, without touching on the literary aspects of the story, it raises general questions of principle, I shall not be sinning against the etiquette if I allow myself to continue our conversation.

In the first place, I, like you, do not like literature of the kind we are discussing.[29] As a reader and "a private resident" I am glad to avoid it, but if you ask my honest and sincere opinion about it, I shall say that it is still an open question whether it has a right to exist, and no one has yet settled it [. . .]. Neither you nor I, nor all the critics in the world, have any trustworthy data that would give them the right to reject such literature. I do not know which are right: Homer, Shakespeare, Lope de Vega, and, speaking generally, the ancients who were not afraid to rummage in the "muck heap," but were morally far more stable than we are, or the modern writers, priggish on paper but coldly cynical in their souls and in life. I do not know which has bad taste—the Greeks who were not ashamed to describe love as it really is in beautiful nature, or the readers of Gaboriau, Marlitz, Pierre Bobo [P. D. Boborykin]. Like the problems of non-resistance to evil, of free will, etc., this question can only be settled in the future. We can only refer to it, but are not competent to decide it. Reference to Turgenev and Tolstoy—who avoided the "muck heap"—does not throw light on the question. Their

---

[29] That is, popular and racy.

63

fastidiousness does not prove anything; why, before them there was a generation of writers who regarded as dirty not only accounts of "the dregs and scum," but even descriptions of peasants and of officials below the rank of titular councilor. Besides, one period, however brilliant, does not entitle us to draw conclusions in favor of this or that literary tendency. Reference to the demoralizing effects of the literary tendency we are discussing does not decide the question either. Everything in this world is relative and approximate. There are people who can be demoralized even by children's books, and who read with particular pleasure the piquant passages in the Psalms and in Solomon's Proverbs, while there are others who become only the purer from closer knowledge of the filthy side of life. Political and social writers, lawyers, and doctors who are initiated into all the mysteries of human sinfulness are not reputed to be immoral; realistic writers are often more moral than archimandrites. And, finally, no literature can outdo real life in its cynicism; a wine-glassful won't make a man drunk when he has already emptied a barrel. [. . .]

2. That the world swarms with "dregs and scum" is perfectly true. Human nature is imperfect, and it would therefore be strange to see none but righteous ones on earth. But to think that the duty of literature is to unearth the pearl from the refuse heap means to reject literature itself. "Artistic" literature is only "art" in so far as it paints life as it really is. Its vocation is to be absolutely true and honest. To narrow down its function to the particular task of finding "pearls" is as deadly for it as it would be to make Levitan[30] draw a tree without including the dirty bark and the yellow leaves. I agree that "pearls" are a good thing, but then a writer is not a confectioner, not a provider of cosmetics, not an entertainer; he is a man bound, under contract, by his sense of duty and his conscience; having put his hand to the plow he mustn't turn back, and, however distasteful, he must conquer his squeamishness and soil his imagination with the dirt of life. He is just like any ordinary reporter. What would you say if a newspaper correspondent out of a feeling of fastidiousness or from a wish to please his readers would describe only honest mayors, high-minded ladies, and virtuous railway contractors?

To a chemist nothing on earth is unclean. A writer must be as objective as a chemist, he must lay aside his personal subjective standpoint and must understand that muck heaps play a very respectable

---

[30] The landscape painter Isaak Levitan was a friend of Chekhov and of Kiseleva.

part in a landscape, and that the evil passions are as inherent in life as the good ones. [. . .]

4. I confess I seldom commune with my conscience when I write. This is due to habit and the brevity of my work. And so when I express this or that opinion about literature, I do not take myself into account. [. . .]

The fate of literature would be sad indeed if it were at the mercy of individual views. That is the first thing. Secondly, there is no police which could consider itself competent in literary matters. I agree that one can't dispense with the reins and the whip altogether, for knaves find their way even into literature, but no thinking will discover a better police for literature than the critics and the author's own conscience. People have been trying to discover such a police since the creation of the world, but they have found nothing better. [. . .]

I have written a play on four sheets of paper.[31] It will take fifteen to twenty minutes to act. [. . .] It is much better to write small things than big ones: they are unpretentious and successful. . . . What more would you have? I wrote my play in an hour and five minutes. I began another, but have not finished it, for I have no time.
—to Maria Kiseleva, January 14, 1887 [CG]

★

The first chapter [of Henry David Thoreau's *Walden*, in Russian translation] promises a great deal; he has ideas, freshness and original-ity, but he is hard to read. The architecture and composition are impossible. Ideas, beautiful and ugly, light and cumbrous, are piled on top of each other, crowded together, squeezing the juice out of each other, and any moment the pressure may make them squeal.
—to Vladimir Korolenko, October 17, 1887 [SK-1]

★

When I was still studying the history of literature I was familiar with a phenomenon that I made into a law: all Russian verse-writers can write prose well. You would not succeed in removing this conviction from my mind, and it did not leave me while I was reading your prose. Perhaps I am wrong, but Lermontov's "Taman" and Pushkin's *The Captain's Daughter*—not to speak of the prose of many other

---

[31] "Kalkhas," retitled as "Swansong."

poets—prove the close relation between the best Russian poetry and fine prose. [. . .]

As to contributions to newspapers and illustrated magazines, I fully agree with you. Is it not the same whether a nightingale sings in a tree or a bush? The idea that talented people must work only for the large magazines is narrow-minded; it is like the attitude of a chinovnik [civil service worker], and is as harmful as any other prejudice. It did have a certain justification when real personalities, like [Vissarion] Belinsky and [Aleksandr] Herzen, were at the head of publications, and when they, in addition to remuneration, used to influence, guide, and teach. But now, when petty groups and yokels are in charge of publications, the longing for the imposing periodicals is beneath criticism, and the sole difference between the large magazine and the low-priced newspaper is a quantitative one, i.e., one that does not merit attention and consideration from the artist's point of view. In only one case is it essential to co-operate with the large magazines:— a long work cannot be broken up into bits and must be published as a whole. I shall send long works to the thick magazines, and shall print the short things wherever the wind and my will lead me.
—to Yakov Polonsky, January 18, 1888 [LF]

*

I have had a letter from Leman. He tells me that "we" (that is, all of you Petersburg people) "have agreed to print advertisements about each other's work on our books," invites me to join, and warns me that among the elect may be included "only such persons as have a certain degree of solidarity with us." I wrote to say that I agreed, and asked him how he came to know with whom I have solidarity and with whom I have not? How full of stuffy twaddle you are in Petersburg! Aren't you really stifled by such words as "solidarity," "unity of young writers," "community of interests," and so on? I understand solidarity and that sort of thing on the stock exchange, in politics, in matters of religion (sects), etc., but the solidarity of young writers is impossible and unnecessary. . . . We cannot think and feel in the same way; our aims are different, or we have no aims at all, we know one another little or not at all, and consequently, there is nothing to which your solidarity can be securely attached. . . . And is it necessary? No. To help your colleague, to respect his personality and his work, not to gossip about him, not to be envious of him, not to lie to him, and not to act the hypocrite toward him—to do all this one need not be so much a young writer as simply a man. . . . Let us be ordinary men, let us treat everybody alike, then we will not need an artificially concocted solidarity. But the insistent seeking for private, professional, clique solidarity of the kind you want, will, against our wish, give rise to spying on one another, to suspicions, control, and we ourselves will become something like the Jesuits in our relations with one another. . . . I, dear Jean, have no solidarity with you, but I promise you, for the rest of your life, full freedom as an artist: that is, you may write whatever you wish, and in whatever fashion you please, you may reason, if you like, à la Koreisha; you may change your convictions a thousand times, etc., etc., and my human relations with you will not change the least bit, and on the jackets of my books I shall always publish advertisements of your works.

I can promise the same to all of my colleagues, and I should not like to be treated otherwise. As I see it, these are the truly normal relations. Only when they exist, can respect and even friendship and sympathy be possible in difficult moments of our lives.
—to Ivan Leont'ev (Shcheglov), May 3, 1888 [LF]

★

It seems to me that the writer of fiction should not try to solve such questions as those of God, pessimism, etc. His business is but to describe those who have been speaking or thinking about God and pessimism, how, and under what circumstances. The artist should be, not the judge of his characters and their conversations, but only an unbiased witness. . . . My business is merely to be talented, i.e., to be able to distinguish between important and unimportant statements, to be able to illuminate the characters and speak their language. . . . The time has come for writers, especially those who are artists, to admit that in this world one cannot make anything out, just as Socrates once admitted it, just as Voltaire admitted it. The mob think they know and understand everything; the more stupid they are, the wider, I think, do they conceive their horizon to be. And if an artist in whom the crowd has faith decides to declare that he understands nothing of what he sees—this in itself constitutes a considerable clarity in the realm of thought, and a great step forward.
—to Aleksei Suvorin, May 30, 1888 [LF]

★

In conversation with my literary colleagues I always insist that it is not the artist's business to solve problems that require a specialist's knowledge. It is a bad thing if a writer tackles a subject he does not understand. We have specialists for dealing with special questions: it is their business to judge of the commune, of the future, of capitalism, of the evils of drunkenness, of boots, of the diseases of women. An artist must judge only of what he understands, his field is just as limited as that of any other specialist—I repeat this and insist on it always. That in his sphere there are no questions, but only answers, can be maintained only by those who have never written and have had no experience of thinking in images. An artist observes, selects, guesses, combines—and this in itself presupposes a problem: unless he had set himself a problem from the very first there would be nothing to conjecture and nothing to select. To put it briefly, I will end by using the language of psychiatry: if one denies that creative work involves problems and purposes, one must admit that an artist creates without premeditation or intention, in a state of aberration; therefore, if an author boasted to me of having written a novel without a preconceived design, under a sudden inspiration, I should call him mad.

You are right in demanding that an artist should take an intelligent attitude to his work, but you confuse two things: solving a problem and stating a problem correctly.

It is only the second that is obligatory for the artist. In [Tolstoy's] *Anna Karenina* and [Pushkin's] *Eugene Onegin* not a single problem is solved, but they satisfy you completely because all the problems in these works are correctly stated. It is the business of the judge to put the right questions, but the answers must be given by the jury according to their own lights.
—to Aleksei Suvorin, October 27, 1888 [LF]

*

You write that one ought to work not for the critics but for the public, that it is too early for me to complain. It is pleasant to think that you work for the public, certainly, but how am I to know that I really work for the public? I myself am not fully satisfied with my work. Thanks to its stinginess and something else, the public (I did not call it base), is not straightforward in its attitude toward us; it is insincere; you will never hear truth from it, and therefore you will not discover whether it needs me or not. It is too soon for me to complain, but it is not and never will be early to ask oneself: do I occupy myself with work or with nonsense? Criticism is silent, the public lies, while my instinct tells me that I am busy with nonsense and trifles. Do I complain? I do not recall the tone in which my letter was written, but if it is so, then I complain not for myself alone, but for all our fraternity, which seems to me forever deserving of pity. [. . .]

I do not like realistic novelists to slander women, but I dislike it even more when they lift woman. by the shoulders—as Yuzhin does—and try to show that even if she is worse than man, yet man is a scoundrel and woman an angel.

—to Aleksei Suvorin, December 26, 1888 [LF]

*

"A hero, a heroine, stage effects are required. But in life, after all, people are not shooting themselves, hanging themselves, declaring their love every minute. And they're not saying clever things every minute. They do more eating, drinking, courting, saying inanities. And that needs to be seen on stage. The sort of play needs to be created where people arrive, leave, lunch, chat about the weather, play bridge . . . not because the author has to have it that way but because that's how it happens in real life. [. . .] There's no need to cram it into any sort of framework. You need for life to be as it is and for people to be as they are, not stilted."

—in conversation on "new dramatic forms" with Daniel Gorodetsky, ca. 1889 [BB]

*

Did you really not like [Tolstoy's] "Kreutzer Sonata"? I don't say it is a work of genius for all time, of that I am no judge; but to my thinking, among the mass of all that is written now, here and abroad, one scarcely could find anything else as powerful both in the gravity of its conception and the beauty of its execution. To say nothing of its artistic merits, which in places are striking, one must be grateful to the novel, if only because it is keenly stimulating to thought. As one reads it, one can scarcely refrain from crying out: "That's true," or "That's absurd." It is true it has some very annoying defects. Apart from all those you enumerate, it has one for which one cannot readily forgive the author—that is, the audacity with which Tolstoy holds

forth about what he doesn't know and is too obstinate to care to understand. Thus his statements about syphilis, foundling hospitals, the aversion of women for the sexual relation, and so on, are not merely open to dispute, but show him up as an ignoramus who has not, in the course of his long life, taken the trouble to read two or three books written by specialists. But yet these defects fly away like feathers in the wind; one simply does not notice them in face of the real worth of the story, or, if one notices them, it is only with a little vexation that the story has not escaped the fate of all the works of man, all imperfect and never free from blemish.
—to Aleksei Pleshcheev, February 15, 1890 [CG]

*

And as regards the word "art," I fear it as merchants' wives fear a Sodom rain of brimstone. When people talk to me of the artistic and the anti-artistic, of that which is theatrical and non-theatrical, of tendency, realism, etc., I become confused, consent irresolutely, and answer with platitudinous half-truths that are not worth a penny. I divide all literary works into two classes: those that I like and those that I do not like. I have no other criterion, and if you were to ask me why I like Shakespeare and dislike Zlatovratsky, I should be unable to answer. Perhaps in time, when I become wiser, I shall acquire a criterion, but meanwhile, all this talk about "artistry" only tires me and seems to me only the continuation of the same scholastic discourses with which people wearied themselves in the Middle Ages.
—to Ivan Leont'ev (Shcheglov), March 22, 1890 [LF]

*

You abuse me for objectivity, calling it indifference to good and evil, lack of ideals and ideas, and so on. You would have me, when I describe horse-thieves, say: "Stealing horses is an evil." But that has been known for ages without my saying so. Let the jury judge them; it's my job simply to show what sort of people they are. I write: you are dealing with horse-thieves, so let me tell you that they are not beggars but well-fed people, that they are people of a special cult, and that horse-stealing is not simply theft but a passion. Of course it would be pleasant to combine art with a sermon, but for me personally it is extremely difficult and almost impossible, owing to the conditions of technique. You see, to depict horse-thieves in seven hundred lines I must all the time speak and think in their tone and feel in their spirit; otherwise, if I introduce subjectivity, the image becomes blurred and the story will not be as compact as all short stories ought to be. When I write, I reckon entirely upon the reader to add for himself the subjective elements that are lacking in the story.

—to Aleksei Suvorin, April 1, 1890 [LF]

★

Boborykin came to see me. He also dreams. He told me he wanted to write a sort of physiology of the Russian novel, its origin here, and its natural course of development. While he was talking I could not rid myself of the thought that I had before me a maniac, a literary maniac who puts literature above anything else in life. In Moscow I so rarely see genuine writers that the talk with Boborykin seemed like heavenly manna, although I do not believe in the physiology of the novel and its natural process of development—that is, a physiology may exist in nature, but I do not believe that with the existing methods it can be grasped. Boborykin dismisses Gogol with both hands and refuses to consider him as the ancestor of Turgenev, Goncharov, Tolstoy. . . . He places him apart, outside the channel in which the Russian novel has flowed. Now, I can't admit that. Once one takes the standpoint of natural development, it is impossible to place outside the channel not only Gogol, but even a dog's barking, for all things in nature influence one another, and even the fact that I have just sneezed is not without its influence on surrounding nature.

—to Aleksei Suvorin, November 30, 1891 [SK-1]

★

It is not difficult to understand you, and you unjustly accuse yourself of obscurity. You are a real drinker and I have treated you to sweet lemonade, and you, in giving it its due, justly observe that there is no spirit in it. There is indeed missing in our work the alcohol which would intoxicate and subdue; and that you make quite clear. Why is it missing? Leaving aside my "Ward No. 6" and myself, let us discuss the matter generally, for that is more interesting. Let us discuss the general causes, if it won't bore you, and let us take a whole epoch.

Tell me frankly, now, who of my contemporaries, that is, men between the ages of 30 and 45, have given the world even one drop of alcohol? Are not Korolenko, Nadson, and all the playwrights of today mere lemonade? Have Repin's and Shishkin's pictures turned your head? Charming, talented, you are delighted, and yet you are none the less conscious that you want to smoke. Science and technology are having a great time now; but for our writing fraternity it is a flabby, miserable, and dull time. We ourselves are sour and dull and able to beget only rubber dummies, yet Stasov, whom nature has enriched with the rare gift of getting drunk even on slops, does not see it. The causes of this are not in our stupidity, not in our lack of talent, nor in our impudence, as Burenin thinks, but in a disease which for an artist is worse than syphilis and impotence. . . .

Remember that the writers whom we call eternal or simply good and who intoxicate us have one common and very important characteristic: they get somewhere, and they summon you there, and you feel, not with your mind, but with your whole being, that they have a certain purpose and, like the ghost of Hamlet's father, do not come and excite the imagination for nothing. Some—it depends on their caliber—have immediate objects: abolition of serfdom, liberation of the country, politics, beauty or simply vodka, like Denis Davydov; others have remote aims: God, the life beyond, the happiness of mankind, and so on. The best of them are realistic and paint life as it is, but because every line is permeated, as with a juice, by awareness of a purpose, you feel, besides life as it is, also life as it ought to be, and this captivates you. And we?

We! We paint life as it is, and beyond that—no "gee-up" nor "gee-down." Beyond that, even if you lashed us with whips, we could not go. We have neither immediate nor remote aims, and in our souls a great emptiness. We have no politics, we do not believe in revolution, we have no God, we are not afraid of ghosts, and I personally have no fear even of death and blindness. He who desires nothing, hopes for nothing, and is afraid of nothing, cannot be an artist. Whether it is a disease or not—the name doesn't matter; but it must be owned our situation is worse than bad. I do not know what we shall become in ten or twenty years—perhaps the circumstances will have changed by that time—but for the time being it would be rash to expect of us anything really good, apart from whether we have talent or not. We write mechanically, submitting ourselves to the long-established custom in accordance with which some are employed in offices, others in trade, others in literature.

You and Grigorovich think that I am clever. Yes, I am at least clever enough not to hide my disease from myself, nor to lie to myself, nor to cover up my emptiness with borrowed rags, such as the ideals of the '60s and so on. I shall not, like Garshin, throw myself down a flight of stairs, but neither am I going to delude myself with hopes of a better future. I am not to blame for my disease, nor am I called upon to cure myself, since this disease has, it must be supposed, some good purpose of its own hidden from us, and has not been sent in vain.
—to Aleksei Suvorin, November 25, 1892 [SK-1]

★

If you want insincerity, there are a million poods of it in Smirnova-Sazonova's letter. "The greatest wonder is man himself, and we shall never tire of studying him . . ." or "The aim of life . . . is life itself . . ." or "I believe in life, in its bright moments, for which we not only can, but must live; I believe in man, in the good part of his soul," etc. Is all this really sincere, and does it mean anything? It is not an opinion, but mere gabble. She underscores "can" and "must," because she is afraid to talk of that which is, and of which one must take account. Let her in the beginning say what there is, and then I will listen to what can and must be. She believes in "life," and that means that she believes in nothing if she is clever, or that she believes in the God of the muzhiks, and crosses herself in the dark, if she is a grandma.
—to Aleksei Suvorin, December 3, 1892 [LF]

★

If the nature of literary work depended only upon the good will of the author, then, you may believe it, we would count good writers by the tens and hundreds.
—to I. I. Ostrovsky, February 11, 1893 [LF]

★

[. . .] if a writer describes a person psychically ill, it does not follow that he is ill himself. I wrote "The Black Monk" in no gloomy frame of mind but after cold deliberation. I simply had a desire to describe mania grandiosa. The monk rushing across the field was a dream; on

waking in the morning I told it to Misha [Chekhov's youngest
brother, Mikhail]. So you can tell Anna Ivanovna [Suvorin's wife]
that poor Anton Pavlovich is not yet mad, thank heaven, but that
he eats a lot at supper and therefore sees monks in his sleep.
—to Aleksei Suvorin, January 25, 1894 [SK-1]

*

It sometimes happens that one passes a third-class refreshment room
and sees a cold fish, cooked long before, and wonders carelessly who
wants that unappetizing fish. And yet undoubtedly that fish is wanted,
and will be eaten, and there are people who will think it nice. One
may say the same of the works of [Kazimir] Barantsevich. He is a
bourgeois writer, writing for the unsophisticated public who travel
third class. For that public Tolstoy and Turgenev are too luxurious,
too aristocratic, somewhat alien, and not easily digested. There is a
public which eats salt beef and horse-radish sauce with relish, and
does not care for artichokes and asparagus. Put yourself at its point
of view, imagine the gray, dreary courtyard, the educated ladies who
look like cooks, the smell of paraffin, the scantiness of interests and
tasks—and you will understand Barantsevich and his readers. He is
colorless; that is partly because the life he describes lacks color. He
is false, because bourgeois writers cannot help being false. They are
vulgar writers perfected. The vulgarians sin together with their public, while the bourgeois are hypocritical with it and flatter its narrow
virtues.
—to Aleksei Suvorin, August 15, 1894 [LF]

*

Verse is not in my line. I have never written poetry; my mind refuses
to memorize poetry, and I can only take hold of it like a muzhik,
but I cannot state definitely why it pleases me or wearies me. Some
time ago I tried to get in touch with poets and to set my views before
them, but nothing came of it, and I soon gave the matter up, like a
man who means well, but who cannot express his ideas in clear and
definite form. Now I usually confine myself to writing," I like this,"
or, "I do not like it." Your poem I like.
  As to the story you are writing, that is a different matter, and I am
ready to pass judgment on it to the extent of twenty sheets of paper;
if you send it to me and ask me to give you my opinion, I shall read

it with pleasure. I shall answer you with some definiteness, and shall feel free.

—to Aleksandr Zhirkevich, March 3, 1895 [LF]

★

I am wading through *The Polonecki Family*, by [Henryk] Sienkiewicz. It is clotted Polish Easter-cake made with saffron. [. . .] It is clear that Sienkiewicz has not read Tolstoy and knows nothing of Nietzsche; he blabbers about hypnotism like a shopkeeper, but for all that every page is sprinkled with Rubens, Borghese, Correggio, Botticelli—and this to show off his erudition before the bourgeois reader and to make an insulting gesture on the sly at materialism. The purpose of the novel is to lull the bourgeoisie in its golden dreams. Be true to your wife, pray with her from the prayer book, make money, love sport—and all is well with you in this world and in the world to come. The bourgeoisie is very fond of the so-called "positive types" and of novels with happy endings, for they set the bourgeoisie at ease with the idea that one may grub money and preserve one's virtue, that one may be a beast and at the same time be happy.

—to Aleksei Suvorin, April 13, 1895 [SK-1]

★

My autobiography? I have a disease—*Autobiographophobia*. To read any sort of details about myself, and still more to write them for print, is a veritable torture to me. On a separate sheet I send a few facts, very bald, but I can do no more. . . .

I, A. P. Chekhov, was born on the 17th of January, 1860, at Taganrog. I was educated first in the Greek School near the church of Tsar Konstantin; then in the Taganrog High School. In 1879 I entered Moscow University in the Faculty of Medicine. I had at the time only a slight idea of the Faculties in general, and chose the Faculty of Medicine I don't remember on what grounds, but did not regret my choice afterwards. I began in my first year to publish stories in the weekly journals and newspapers, and these literary pursuits had, early in the eighties, acquired a permanent professional character. In 1888 I took the Pushkin Prize. In 1890 I traveled to the Island of Sakhalin, to write afterwards a book upon our penal colony and prisons there. Not counting reviews, feuilletons, paragraphs, and all that I have written from day to day for the newspapers, which it would be difficult now to seek out and collect, I have, during my twenty years of literary work, published more than three hundred signatures of print, of tales and novels. I have also written plays for the stage.

I have no doubt that the study of medicine has had an important influence on my literary work; it has considerably enlarged the sphere of my observation, has enriched me with knowledge the true value of which for me as a writer can only be understood by one who is himself a doctor. It has also had a guiding influence, and it is probably due to my close association with medicine that I have succeeded in avoiding many mistakes.

Familiarity with the natural sciences and with scientific method has always kept me on my guard, and I have always tried, where it was possible, to be consistent with the facts of science, and where it was impossible I have preferred not to write at all. I may observe in passing that the conditions of artistic creation do not always admit of complete harmony with the facts of science. It is impossible to represent upon the stage a death from poisoning exactly as it takes place in reality. But harmony with the facts of science must be felt even under those conditions—i.e., it must be clear to the reader or spectator that this is only due to the conditions of art, and that he has to do with a writer who understands.

I do not belong to the class of literary men who take up a skeptical attitude towards science; and to the class of those who rush into everything with only their own imagination to go upon, I should not like to belong.
—to Grigory Rossolimo, October 11, 1899 [LF]

★

I don't know how to write for children; I write for them once in ten years, and so-called children's books I don't like and don't believe in. Children ought only to be given what is suitable also for grown-up people. Andersen, "The Frigate Pallada," Gogol, are easily read by children and also by grown-up people. Books should not be written for children, but one ought to know how to choose from what has been written for grown-up people—that is, from real works of art. To be able to select drugs and to administer them in suitable doses, is more direct and consistent than trying to invent a special remedy for the patient because he is a child. Forgive the medical comparison.
—Grigory Rossolimo, January 21, 1900 [LF]

★

. . . while Tolstoy is in literature it is easy and pleasant to be a writer; even to be aware that one has done nothing and is doing nothing is not so terrible, since Tolstoy does enough for all. His work serves as the justification of all the hopes and anticipations built upon literature. Thirdly, Tolstoy stands firmly, his authority is immense, and while he lives, bad taste in literature, banality of every kind, impudent or lachrymose, all the bristling, exasperated vanities will remain far away, deep in the shade. His moral authority alone is capable of maintaining on a certain height the so-called literary moods and currents. Without him they would all be a shepherdless flock, or a hodge-podge in which it would be difficult to make out anything.

—to Mikhail Menshikov, January 28, 1900 [SK-1]

★

"Critics are like horse-flies which prevent the horse from plowing. The horse works, all its muscles drawn tight like the strings on a double-bass, and a fly settles on its flanks and tickles and buzzes . . . he has to twitch his skin and swish his tail. And what does the fly buzz about? It scarcely knows itself; simply because it is restless and wants to proclaim: 'Look, I too am living on the earth. See, I can buzz, too, buzz about anything.' For over twenty years I have read criticisms of my stories, and I do not remember a single remark of any value or one word of valuable advice. Only once Skabichevsky [a popular radical critic] wrote something which made an impression on me. He said I would die in a ditch, drunk."

—in conversation with Maxim Gorky, ca. 1900 [SK-3]

★

[. . .] theaters for the people as well as literature for the people is all silliness and candy. Gogol is not to be lowered to the people, but the people raised up to Gogol.

—to Vladimir Nemirovich-Danchenko, November 2, 1903 [SK-1]

★

"Our present-day hotheads want to grasp what is scientifically ungrasp-able, to grasp the physical laws of creative art, to detect the general law, and formulae by which an artist, who feels them instinctively, creates musical compositions, landscapes, novels, etc. The physiology of creative activity does probably exist in nature, but the dreamings about that physiology should be cut short at the very start. If the critics take their stand on scientific ground, no good can come of it; they will waste a dozen years, write a lot of rubbish, make the ques-tion still more confusing—and get nowhere. To think scientifically is good in everything, but the trouble is that scientific speculation about creative work will in the long run, willy-nilly, be reduced to hunting for 'cells' or 'centers,' which control the creative faculty; and then some stolid German will locate those cells somewhere in the temporal region of the brain, a second German will disagree with him . . . and a stupid craze will obsess Russia for three years, provid-ing a living for blockheads and filling sensible people with nothing but irritation."

—in conversation with Yuriy Sobolev, no date [SK-2]

IV.

FICTIONAL WRITERS

ALTHOUGH COMMITTED TO the principle of not writing about himself in his fiction, Chekhov acknowledged that his own experiences infused those of his characters. Chekhov's depictions of writers in his stories and plays are rarely flattering, often teasing, and always revealing of the fragility and anxiety of literary work. These excerpts from his stories and plays are laid out in chronological order by publication date.

EASTER EVE

In the figure of the eulogized monk, Nikolai, Chekhov pays tribute to the kind of writer and person that he particularly admired, someone who exalted goodness by writing canticles, "hymns of praise." Nikolai's mourner is his fellow monk, Ieronim. The narrator is a visitor who loves Easter music—much as Chekhov, a nonbeliever, did. Ieronim is serving as a bargeman for the monastery's visitors.

"He had a gift for writing hymns of praise," he said. "It was a marvel, sir; you couldn't call it anything else! You would be amazed if I tell you about it. Our Father Archimandrite comes from Moscow, the Father Sub-Prior studied at the Kazan academy, we have wise monks and elders, but, would you believe it, no one could write them; while Nikolai, a simple monk, a deacon, had not studied anywhere, and had not even any outer appearance of it, but he wrote them! A marvel! A real marvel!" Ieronim clasped his hands and, completely forgetting the rope, went on eagerly: "The Father Sub-Prior has great difficulty in composing sermons; when he wrote the history of the monastery he worried all the brotherhood and drove

79

a dozen times to town, while Nikolai wrote canticles! Hymns of
praise! That's a very different thing from a sermon or a history!"

"Is it difficult to write them?" I asked.

"There's great difficulty!" Ieronim wagged his head. "You can do
nothing by wisdom and holiness if God has not given you the gift. The
monks who don't understand argue that you only need to know
the life of the saint for whom you are writing the hymn, and to
make it harmonize with the other hymns of praise. But that's a mistake, sir. Of course, anyone who writes canticles must know the life
of the saint to perfection, to the least trivial detail. To be sure, one must
make them harmonize with the other canticles and know where to
begin and what to write about. [. . .] but the lives of the saints and
conformity with the others is not what matters; what matters is the
beauty and sweetness of it. Everything must be harmonious, brief
and complete. There must be in every line softness, graciousness and
tenderness; not one word should be harsh or rough or unsuitable. It
must be written so that the worshipper may rejoice at heart and weep,
while his mind is stirred and he is thrown into a tremor. [. . .]

"To think that a man should find words like those! Such a power
is a gift from God! For brevity he packs many thoughts into one
phrase, and how smooth and complete it all is! [. . .] 'Light-radiating!'
There is no such word in conversation or in books, but you see he
invented it, he found it in his mind! Apart from the smoothness and
grandeur of language, sir, every line must be beautified in every way,
there must be flowers and lightning and wind and sun and all the
objects of the visible world. And every exclamation ought to be put
so as to be smooth and easy for the ear. 'Rejoice, thou flower of
heavenly growth!' comes in the hymn to Nikolai the Wonder-worker.
It's not simply 'heavenly flower,' but 'flower of heavenly growth.' It's
smoother so and sweet to the ear. That was just as Nikolai wrote it!
Exactly like that! I can't tell you how he used to write!"

. . . "What did he write them for?"

"Chiefly for his own comfort." [. . .]

—published April 13, 1886 [CG]

THE PRIVY COUNCILOR

The narrator recalls his childhood and a summertime visit from his mysterious and dignified uncle.

For the first two or three weeks we did not see my uncle often. For days together he sat in his own room working, in spite of the flies and the heat. His extraordinary capacity for sitting as though glued to his table produced upon us the effect of an inexplicable conjuring trick. To us idlers, knowing nothing of systematic work, his industry seemed simply miraculous. Getting up at nine, he sat down to his table, and did not leave it till dinner-time; after dinner he set to work again, and went on till late at night.

The work consisted in his writing with one hand while he turned over the leaves of a book with the other, and, strange to say, he kept moving all over—swinging his leg as though it were a pendulum, whistling, and nodding his head in time. He had an extremely careless and frivolous expression all the while, as though he were not working, but playing tic-tac-toe.

—published May 6, 1886 [CG]

81

HUSH!

Chekhov seems to have had in mind his brother Aleksandr for this picture of family life.

"Shattered, soul-weary, a sick load of misery on the heart . . . and then to sit down and write. And this is called life! How is it nobody has described the agonizing discord in the soul of a writer who has to amuse the crowd when his heart is heavy or to shed tears at the word of command when his heart is light? I must be playful, coldly unconcerned, witty, but what if I am weighed down with misery, what if I am ill, or my child is dying or my wife in anguish!"

He says this, brandishing his fists and rolling his eyes. . . . Then he goes into the bedroom and wakes his wife.

"Nadya," he says, "I am sitting down to write. . . . Please don't let anyone interrupt me. I can't write with children crying or cooks snoring. . . . See, too, that there's tea and . . . steak or something. . . . You know that I can't write without tea. . . . Tea is the one thing that gives me the energy for my work." [. . .]

Ivan Yegorich throws himself back in his chair, and closing his eyes concentrates himself on his subject. He hears his wife shuffling about in her slippers and splitting shavings to heat the samovar. [. . .]

Like a girl who has been presented with a costly fan, he spends a long time coquetting, grimacing, and posing to himself before he writes the title. . . . He presses his temples, he wriggles, and draws his legs up under his chair as though he were in pain, or half closes his eyes languidly like a cat on the sofa. At last, not without hesitation, he stretches out his hand towards the inkstand, and with an expression as though he were signing a death-warrant, writes the title. [. . .]

He writes till four o'clock and would readily have written till six if his subject had not been exhausted. Coquetting and posing to himself and the inanimate objects about him, far from any indiscreet,

82

critical eye, tyrannizing and domineering over the little anthill that fate has put in his power are the honey and the salt of his existence. And how different is this despot here at home from the humble, meek, dull-witted little man we are accustomed to see in the editor's offices!

"I am so exhausted that I am afraid I shan't sleep . . ." he says as he gets into bed. "Our work, this cursed, ungrateful hard labor, exhausts the soul even more than the body. . . . I had better take some bromide. . . . God knows, if it were not for my family I'd throw up the work. . . . To write to order! It is awful."

He sleeps till twelve or one o'clock in the day, sleeps a sound, healthy sleep. . . . Ah! how he would sleep, what dreams he would have, how he would spread himself if he were to become a well-known writer, an editor, or even a sub-editor!

"He has been writing all night," whispers his wife with a scared expression on her face. "Sh!"

No one dares to speak or move or make a sound. His sleep is something sacred, and the culprit who offends against it will pay dearly for his fault.

"Hush!" floats over the flat. "Hush!"

—published November 15, 1886 [CG]

EXCELLENT PEOPLE

This story is about the disintegration of a sibling relationship. The brother, a critic, has been accustomed to his sister's uncritical admiration. Due to her spiritual conversion to the Tolstoyan movement, she recognizes the severe limitations of her brother's literary pronouncements.

His sister gave up sitting beside his table and gazing reverently at his writing hand, and he felt every evening that behind him on the sofa lay a person who did not agree with him. And his back grew stiff and numb, and there was a chill in his soul. An author's vanity is vindictive, implacable, incapable of forgiveness, and his sister was the first and only person who had laid bare and disturbed that uneasy feeling, which is like a big box of crockery, easy to unpack but impossible to pack up again as it was before.

—published November 22, 1886 [CG]

HOME

Although Chekhov was proud of being professional and writing to order and to deadline, he was amused by and sympathetic to people who were not specialists in the art of storytelling. In this excerpt from one of his most moving and charming stories, a recently widowed father feels at a loss while inventing a story for his seven-year-old son, Seryozha, who has been caught by his governess smoking cigarettes. Yevgeny Petrovich is a trial lawyer.

Yevgeny Petrovich on his free evenings was in the habit of telling Seryozha stories. Like most people engaged in practical affairs, he did not know a single poem by heart, and could not remember a single fairy tale, so he had to improvise. As a rule he began with the stereotyped: "In a certain country, in a certain kingdom," then he heaped up all kinds of innocent nonsense and had no notion as he told the beginning how the story would go on, and how it would end. Scenes, characters, and situations were taken at random, impromptu, and the plot and the moral came of itself as it were, with no plan on the part of the story-teller. . . .

Seryozha was very fond of this improvisation, and the prosecutor noticed that the simpler and the less ingenious the plot, the stronger the impression it made on the child. . . .

"Listen," he said, raising his eyes to the ceiling. "Once upon a time, in a certain country, in a certain kingdom, there lived an old, very old emperor with a long gray beard, and . . . and with great gray moustaches like this. Well, he lived in a glass palace which sparkled and glittered in the sun, like a great piece of clear ice. The palace, my boy, stood in a huge garden, in which there grew oranges, you know . . . bergamots, cherries . . . tulips, roses, and lilies-of-the-valley were in flower in it, and birds of different colors sang there. . . . Yes. . . . On the trees there hung little glass bells, and, when the wind blew, they rang so sweetly that one was never tired of hearing them. Glass gives a softer, tenderer note than metals. . . . Well, what next?

85

There were fountains in the garden. . . . Do you remember you saw a fountain at Auntie Sonya's summer villa? Well, there were fountains just like that in the emperor's garden, only ever so much bigger, and the jets of water reached to the top of the highest poplar." [. . .]

Yevgeny Petrovich thought a moment, and went on:

"The old emperor had an only son and heir of his kingdom—a boy as little as you. He was a good boy. He was never naughty, he went to bed early, he never touched anything on the table, and altogether he was a sensible boy. He had only one fault, he used to smoke. . . ."

Seryozha listened attentively, and looked into his father's eyes without blinking.

The prosecutor went on, thinking: "What next?" [. . .]

He spun out a long rigmarole, and ended like this:

"The emperor's son fell ill with consumption through smoking, and died when he was twenty. His infirm and sick old father was left without anyone to help him. There was no one to govern the kingdom and defend the palace. Enemies came, killed the old man, and destroyed the palace, and now there are neither cherries, nor birds, nor little bells in the garden. . . . That's what happened."

This ending struck Yevgeny Petrovich as absurd and naive, but the whole story made an intense impression on Seryozha. Again his eyes were clouded by mournfulness and something like fear; for a minute he looked pensively at the dark window, shuddered, and said, in a sinking voice:

"I am not going to smoke any more. . . ."

When he had said good-night and gone away his father walked up and down the room and smiled to himself.

"They would tell me it was the influence of beauty, artistic form," he meditated. "It may be so, but that's no comfort. It's not the right way, all the same. . . . Why must morality and truth never be offered in their crude form, but only with embellishments, sweetened and gilded like pills? It's not normal. . . . It's falsification . . . deception . . . tricks . . . ."

He thought of the jurymen to whom it was absolutely necessary to make a "speech," of the general public who absorb history only from legends and historical novels, and of himself and how he had gathered an understanding of life not from sermons and laws, but from fables, novels, poems. [. . .]

[*Yevgeny Petrovich concludes*] "There are many deceptions and delusions in nature that serve a purpose."

—published March 7, 1887 [CG]

A PLAY

An aspiring playwright imposes herself on an editor in his office. While Chekhov seems to have never turned down any writer's request to look at their work, this generous reader, Pavel Vassilyevich, regrets giving this playwright his favor.

"I'm a great admirer of your talent and always read your articles with great enjoyment. . . . Don't imagine I'm flattering you—God forbid!—I'm only giving honor where honor is due. . . . I am always reading you . . . always! To some extent I am myself not a stranger to literature—that is, of course . . . I will not venture to call myself an authoress, but . . . still I have added my little quota . . . I have published at different times three stories for children. . . . You have not read them, of course. . . . I have translated a good deal and . . . and my late brother used to write for *The Cause.*"

"To be sure . . . er—er—er——What can I do for you?"

"You see . . . (the lady cast down her eyes and turned redder) I know your talents . . . your views, Pavel Vassilyevich, and I have been longing to learn your opinion, or more exactly . . . to ask your advice. I must tell you I have perpetrated a play, my first-born—*pardon pour l'expression!*—and before sending it to the Censor I should like above all things to have your opinion on it."

Nervously, with the flutter of a captured bird, the lady fumbled in her skirt and drew out a fat manuscript.

Pavel Vassilyevich liked no articles but his own. When threatened with the necessity of reading other people's, or listening to them, he felt as though he were facing the cannon's mouth. Seeing the manuscript he took fright and hastened to say:

"Very good . . . leave it, . . . I'll read it."

"Pavel Vassilyevich," the lady said languishingly, clasping her hands and raising them in supplication, "I know you're busy. . . . Your

87

every minute is precious, and I know you're inwardly cursing me at this moment, but . . . Be kind, allow me to read you my play. . . . Do be so very sweet!"

"I should be delighted . . ." faltered Pavel Vassilyevich; "but, Madam, I'm . . . I'm very busy. . . . I'm . . . I'm obliged to set off this minute."

"Pavel Vassilyevich," moaned the lady and her eyes filled with tears, "I'm asking a sacrifice! I am insolent, I am intrusive, but be magnanimous. Tomorrow I'm leaving for Kazan and I should like to know your opinion today. Grant me half an hour of your attention . . . only one half-hour . . . I implore you!"

Pavel Vassilyevich was cotton-wool at core, and could not refuse. When it seemed to him that the lady was about to burst into sobs and fall on her knees, he was overcome with confusion and muttered helplessly.

"Very well; certainly . . . I will listen . . . I will give you half an hour."

The lady uttered a shriek of joy, took off her hat and settling herself, began to read. At first she read a scene in which a footman and a house maid, tidying up a sumptuous drawing-room, talked at length about their young lady, Anna Sergyevna, who was building a school and a hospital in the village. When the footman had left the room, the maidservant pronounced a monologue to the effect that education is light and ignorance is darkness; then Mme. Murashkin brought the footman back into the drawing-room and set him uttering a long monologue concerning his master, the General, who disliked his daughter's views, intended to marry her to a rich kammer junker, and held that the salvation of the people lay in unadulterated ignorance. Then, when the servants had left the stage, the young lady herself appeared and informed the audience that she had not slept all night, but had been thinking of Valentin Ivanovich, who was the son of a poor teacher and assisted his sick father gratuitously. Valentin had studied all the sciences, but had no faith in friendship nor in love; he had no object in life and longed for death, and therefore she, the young lady, must save him.

Pavel Vassilyevich listened, and thought with yearning anguish of his sofa. He scanned the lady viciously, felt her masculine tenor thumping on his eardrums, understood nothing, and thought:

"The devil sent you . . . as though I wanted to listen to your tosh! It's not my fault you've written a play, is it? My God! what a thick manuscript! What an infliction!"

Pavel Vassilyevich glanced at the wall where the portrait of his wife was hanging and remembered that his wife had asked him to buy and bring to their summer cottage five yards of tape, a pound of cheese, and some tooth-powder.

"I hope I've not lost the pattern of that tape," he thought, "where did I put it? I believe it's in my blue reefer jacket. . . . Those wretched flies have covered her portrait with spots already, I must tell Olga to wash the glass. . . . She's reading the twelfth scene, so we must soon be at the end of the first act. As though inspiration were possible in this heat and with such a mountain of flesh, too! Instead of writing plays she'd much better eat cold vinegar hash and sleep in a cellar. . . ."

"You don't think that monologue's a little too long?" the lady asked suddenly, raising her eyes.

Pavel Vassilyevich had not heard the monologue, and said in a voice as guilty as though not the lady but he had written that monologue:

"No, no, not at all. It's very nice . . ."

The lady beamed with happiness and continued reading [. . .].

Like a man condemned to be executed and convinced of the impossibility of a reprieve, Pavel Vassilyevich gave up expecting the end, abandoned all hope, and simply tried to prevent his eyes from closing, and to retain an expression of attention on his face. . . . The future when the lady would finish her play and depart seemed to him so remote that he did not even think of it.

"Trooo—too—too—too . . ." the lady's voice sounded in his ears. "Troo—too—too . . . sh—sh—sh—sh . . ."

—published June 13, 1887

A Dreary Story: From the Notebook
of an Old Man

*In Chekhov's marvelous and never boring or "dreary" story—Chekhov
insisted on this title when his editor objected—the "old man" of sixty-two
accounts for his life and state of mind. In precise language, he describes his
difficulties writing.*

I still, as in the past, lecture fairly well; I can still, as in the past, hold
the attention of my listeners for a couple of hours. My fervor, the
literary skill of my exposition, and my humor, almost efface the defects
of my voice, though it is harsh, dry, and monotonous as a praying
beggar's. I write poorly. That bit of my brain which presides over the
faculty of authorship refuses to work. My memory has grown weak;
there is a lack of sequence in my ideas, and when I put them on paper
it always seems to me that I have lost the instinct for their organic
connection; my construction is monotonous; my language is poor
and timid. Often I write what I do not mean; I have forgotten the
beginning when I am writing the end. Often I forget ordinary words,
and I always have to waste a great deal of energy in avoiding superfluous
phrases and unnecessary parentheses in my letters, both unmistakable
proofs of a decline in mental activity. And it is noteworthy that the
simpler the letter the more painful the effort to write it. At a scientific
article I feel far more intelligent and at ease than at a letter of
congratulation or a minute of proceedings. Another point: I find it
easier to write German or English than to write Russian. [. . .]

—published November 1889 [CG]

In Moscow

Chekhov mocks the envy that poisons relationships among writers.

When I am told that somebody or other has written a very interesting article, that somebody's play has been successful, that J. won 200 thousand, and that N.'s speech produced a profound impression, I squint knowingly, I become altogether cross-eyed, and say, "I am very glad for his sake, but, then, you know, in '74 he was tried for theft!"

My soul turns into a piece of lead; with all my being I hate him who has been successful, and I continue: "He tortures his wife, and has three mistresses, and is forever giving dinners to the critics. In general he is a real beast. . . . The story is not bad, but without a doubt he stole it somewhere. His want of talent cries to Heaven. Indeed, to speak frankly, I find nothing in particular in the story."

On the other hand, suppose somebody's play has failed, I am tremendously happy, and hasten to take the author's side. "No, gentlemen, no!" I cry. "There is something in the play. At all events, it is literary."

—published in *New Times* (pseudonymously by "Kislyaev"), December 7, 1891 [LF]

THREE YEARS

Kostya is a relatively minor but thoroughly interesting character in Chekhov's fine novella. Yulia Sergeyevna is a young, modest, religious, and unhappily married partner of a dull man.

At first Yulia Sergeyevna did not like Kostya; his bass voice, his phrases such as "Landed him one on the beak," "filth," "produce the samovar," etc., his habit of clinking glasses and making sentimental speeches, seemed to her trivial. But as she got to know him better, she began to feel very much at home with him. He was open with her; he liked talking to her in a low voice in the evening, and even gave her novels of his own composition to read, though these had been kept a secret even from such friends as Laptev and Yartsev. She read these novels and praised them, so that she might not disappoint him, and he was delighted because he hoped sooner or later to become a distinguished author.

In his novels he described nothing but country-house life, though he had only seen the country on rare occasions when visiting friends at a summer villa, and had only been in a real country-house once in his life, when he had been to Volokolamsk on law business. He avoided any love interest as though he were ashamed of it; he put in frequent descriptions of nature, and in them was fond of using such expressions as, "the capricious lines of the mountains, the miraculous forms of the clouds, the harmony of mysterious rhythms . . ." His novels had never been published, and this he attributed to the censorship.

He liked the duties of a lawyer, but yet he considered that his most important pursuit was not the law but these novels.

—published in 1895 [CG]

92

THE SEAGULL

Chekhov wrote The Seagull *in 1895. (See pages 57–58 for his thoughts and anxieties about this play.) One of the major characters is the writer Trigorin, who shares his author's approximate age and degree of fame, although Chekhov, unlike Trigorin, was notably unpretentious. Nina's aspirations may be compared to Elena Shavrova's (see Section I). This dialogue is from Act 2.*

NINA: Good morning, Boris Alexeyevich!

TRIGORIN: Good morning. Circumstances have turned out so unexpectedly that it seems we are setting off today. We are hardly likely to meet again. I am sorry. I don't often have the chance of meeting young girls, youthful and charming; I have forgotten how one feels at eighteen or nineteen and can't picture it to myself, and so the young girls in my stories and novels are usually false. I should like to be in your shoes just for one hour to find out how you think, and altogether what sort of person you are.

NINA: And I should like to be in your shoes.

TRIGORIN: What for?

NINA: To know what it feels like to be a famous, gifted author. What does it feel like to be famous? How does it affect you, being famous?

TRIGORIN: How? No-how, I believe. I have never thought about it. (*After a moment's thought*) It's one of two things: either you exaggerate my fame, or it never is felt at all.

NINA: But if you read about yourself in the newspapers?

TRIGORIN: When they praise me I am pleased, and when they abuse me I feel out of humor for a day or two.

NINA: What a wonderful world! If only you knew how I envy you! How different people's lots in life are! Some can scarcely get through their dull, obscure existence, they are all just like one another, they are all unhappy; while others—you, for instance—you are one out of a million, have an interesting life full of brightness and significance. You are happy.

TRIGORIN: I? (*shrugging his shoulders*). Hm. You talk of fame and happiness, of bright interesting life, but to me all those fine words, if you will forgive my saying so, are just like a sweetmeat which I never taste. You are very young and very good-natured.

NINA: Your life is splendid!

TRIGORIN: What is there particularly nice in it? (*Looks at his watch*) I must go and write directly. Excuse me, I mustn't stay . . . (*laughs*). You have stepped on my favorite corn, as the saying is, and here I am beginning to get excited and a little cross. Let us talk though. We will talk about my splendid bright life. . . . Well, where shall we begin? (*After thinking a little*) There are such things as fixed ideas, when a man thinks day and night for instance, of nothing but the moon. And I have just such a moon. I am haunted day and night by one persistent thought: I ought to be writing, I ought to be writing, I ought. I have scarcely finished one novel when, for some reason, I must begin writing another, then a third, after the third a fourth. I write incessantly, post haste, and I can't write in any other way. What is there splendid and bright in that, I ask you? Oh, it's an absurd life! Here I am with you; I am excited, yet every moment I remember that my unfinished novel is waiting for me. Here I see a cloud that looks like a grand piano. I think that I must put into a story somewhere that a cloud sailed by that looked like a grand piano. There is a scent of heliotrope. I hurriedly make a note: a sickly smell, a widow's flower, to be mentioned in the description of a summer evening. I catch up myself and you at every sentence, every word, and make haste to put those sentences and words away into my literary treasure-house—it may come in useful! When I finish work I race off to the theater or to fishing; if only I could rest in that and forget myself. But no, there's a new subject rolling about in my head like a heavy iron cannon ball, and I am drawn to my writing table and must make haste again to go on writing and writing. And it's always like that, always. And I have no rest from myself, and I feel that I am eating up my own life, and that for the sake of the honey I give to someone in space I am stripping the pollen from my best flowers, tearing up the flowers themselves and trampling on their roots. Don't you think I am mad? Do my friends and acquaintances treat me as though I were sane?

"What are you writing? What are you giving us?" It's the same thing again and again, and it seems to me as though my friends' notice, their praises, their enthusiasm that it's all a sham, that they are deceiving me as an invalid and I am somehow afraid that they will steal up to me from behind, snatch me and carry me off and put me in a mad-house. And in those years, the best years of my youth, when I was beginning, my writing was unmixed torture. A small writer, particularly when he is not successful, seems to himself clumsy, awkward, unnecessary; his nerves are strained and overwrought. He can't resist hanging about people connected with literature and art, unrecognized and unnoticed by anyone, afraid to look anyone boldly in the face, like a passionate gambler without any money. I hadn't seen my reader, but for some reason I always imagined him hostile, and mistrustful. I was afraid of the public, it alarmed me, and when I had to produce my first play it always seemed to me that all the dark people felt hostile and all the fair ones were coldly indifferent. Oh, how awful it was! What agony it was!

NINA: But surely inspiration and the very process of creation give you moments of exalted happiness?

TRIGORIN: Yes. While I am writing I enjoy it. And I like reading my proofs, but . . . as soon as it is published I can't endure it, and I see that it is all wrong, a mistake, that it ought not to have been written at all, and I feel vexed and sick about it . . . (laughing). And the public reads it and says: "Yes, charming, clever. Charming, but very inferior to Tolstoy," or, "It's a fine thing, but Turgenev's Fathers and Children is finer." And it will be the same to my dying day, only charming and clever, charming and clever and nothing more. And when I die my friends, passing by my tomb, will say, "Here lies Trigorin. He was a good writer, but inferior to Turgenev."

NINA: Forgive me, but I refuse to understand you. You are simply spoiled by success.

TRIGORIN: What success? I have never liked myself; I dislike my own work. The worst of it is that I am in a sort of delirium, and often don't understand what I am writing. I love this water here, the trees, the sky. I feel nature, it arouses in me a passionate, irresistible desire to write. But I am not simply a landscape painter; I am also a citizen. I love my native country, my people; I feel that if I am a writer I am in duty bound to write of the people, of their sufferings, of their future, to talk about science and the rights of man and so on, and so on, and I write about everything. I am hurried and flustered, and on all sides they whip me up and are angry with me; I dash about from side to side like a fox beset by hounds. I see life and culture continually getting farther and farther away while I fall farther and farther behind like a peasant too late for the train; and what it comes to is that I feel I can only describe scenes and in everything else I am false to the marrow of my bones.

NINA: You are overworked and have not the leisure nor the desire to appreciate your own significance. You may be dissatisfied with yourself, but for others you are great and splendid! If I were a writer like you, I should give up my whole life to the common herd, but I should know that there could be no greater happiness for them than to rise to my level, and they would harness them-selves to my chariot.

TRIGORIN: My chariot, what next! Am I an Agamemnon, or what? (*Both smile.*)

NINA: For such happiness as being a writer or an artist I would be ready to endure poverty, disappointment, the dislike of those around me; I would live in a garret and eat nothing but rye bread, I would suffer from being dissatisfied with myself, from recognizing my own imperfections, but I should ask in return for fame . . . real, resounding fame. . . . (*covers her face with her hands*). It makes me dizzy. Oh!

—performed and published in 1896 [CG]

BIBLIOGRAPHY

THE VAST MAJORITY of Chekhov's reflections and observations on writing in this collection are from his marvelous letters. Although the only way to read them all is in Russian, there are several excellent collections in English, the best of which is Michael Henry Heim and Simon Karlinsky's *Anton Chekhov's Life and Thought: Selected Letters and Commentary* (1975). Louis S. Friedland's *Letters on the Short Story, the Drama and Other Literary Topics by Anton Chekhov* (1924, republished by Dover in 1966) is a terrific and larger collection of quotations than this one. I have borrowed seventy of Friedland's translations as well as forty-five by Samuel Solomonovich Koteliansky and twenty by the great Constance Garnett. Notably, Garnett translated almost the entirety of the final section's fictional depictions of writers. In a few instances, I have modified the syntax or updated or corrected a translation of a particular word. I have regularized the spelling of all names and adopted American spellings over the British. The two dozen translations not by Friedland, Koteliansky, or Garnett are new ones by me, for the most part checked or corrected by the expert and tactful translator Liv Bliss. Thank you, Liv.

QUOTATION SOURCES

Chekhov, Anton. *Anton Chekhov: Literary and Theatrical Reminiscences.* Translated and edited by S. S. Koteliansky. George Routledge and Sons, 1927. [SK-2]

Chekhov, Anton. *Letters of Anton Tchehov to His Family and Friends.* Translated by Constance Garnett. Macmillan, 1920. [CG]

Chekhov, Anton. *Letters on the Short Story, the Drama and Other Literary Topics by Anton Chekhov.* Translated by Louis S. Friedland. 1924. Reprint, Dover Publications, 1966. [LF]

Chekhov, Anton. *The Life and Letters of Anton Tchekhov*. Translated by S. S. Koteliansky and Philip Tomlinson. Cassell and Company, Ltd., 1925. [SK-1]

Chekhov, Anton. *The Sea-Gull*. Translated by Constance Garnett. Thomas Seltzer, 1924. [CG]

Chekhov, Anton. *The Tales of Chekhov*. Translated by Constance Garnett. 13 volumes. 1916–29. [CG]

Chekhov, A. P. *Polnoe Sobranie Sochineniy i Pisem* [Collected Works and Letters]. 30 volumes [Works in 18 volumes]. Izdatel'stvo "Nauka," 1976. (See also Chehov-Lit.ru.) [BB]

Gorky, Maxim, and Alexander Kuprin and I. A. Bunin. *Reminiscences of Anton Chekhov*. Translated by S. S. Koteliansky and Leonard Woolf. B. W. Huebsch, 1921. [SK-3]

Izmaylov, A. A. "Antosha Chekhonte." 1916. (See also Chehov-Lit.ru.) [BB]

BIOGRAPHY, BACKGROUND, AND COLLECTIONS OF LETTERS

Bartlett, Rosamund. *Chekhov: Scenes from a Life*. The Free Press, 2005.

Blaisdell, Bob. *Chekhov Becomes Chekhov: The Emergence of a Literary Genius: 1886–1887*. Pegasus, 2022.

Bunin, Ivan. *About Chekhov: The Unfinished Symphony*. Edited and translated by Thomas Gaiton Marullo. Northwestern University Press, 2007.

Chekhov, Anton. *A. P. Chekhov o Literature* [A. P. Chekhov on Literature]. 1955.

Chekhov, Anton. *The Lady with the Dog and Other Love Stories*. Edited by Bob Blaisdell. Dover Publications, 2021.

Chekhov, Mikhail. *Anton Chekhov: A Brother's Memoir*. Translated by Eugene Alper. Palgrave Macmillan, 2010.

Coope, John. *Doctor Chekhov: A Study in Literature and Medicine*. Cross Publishing, 1997.

Finke, Michael C. *Freedom from Violence and Lies: Anton Chekhov's Life and Writings*. Reaktion, 2021.

Gromova, L. D., and N. I. Gitovich. *Letopis' Zhizni i tvorchestva A. P. Chekhova* [Chronicle of the Life and Work of A. P. Chekhov]. Nasledie, 2000.

Heim, Michael Henry, with Simon Karlinsky. *Anton Chekhov's Life and Thought: Selected Letters and Commentary*. University of California Press, 1975.

Lederer, Sidonie K. *The Selected Letters of Anton Chekhov*. Edited with an introduction by Lillian Hellman. McGraw-Hill, 1965.

Kataev, Vladimir B. *A. P. Chekhov Entsiklopediya* [A. P. Chekhov Encyclopedia]. Prosveshchenie, 2011.

Kostin, A. L. *A. P. Chekhov v Vospominaniyakh Sovremennikov* [A. P. Chekhov in Contemporaries' Reminiscences]. Gelios, 2004.

Magarshack, David. *Chekhov: A Life*. Grove Press, 1952.

McVay, Gordon. *Chekhov: A Life in Letters*. The Folio Society, 1994.

Mudrick, Marvin. "Chekhov." In *The Man in the Machine*. Horizon Press, 1977.

Rayfield, Donald. *Anton Chekhov: A Life*. 2nd ed. Garnett Press, 2021.

Rubina, Dina. Preface to *Chekhov's Letters: Biography, Context, Poetics*. Edited by Carol Apollonio and Radislav Lapushin. Lexington Books, 2018.

Simmons, Ernest J. *Chekhov: A Biography*. Atlantic Monthly Press, 1962.

Ural'skiy, Mark. *Chekhov i Evrei* [Chekhov and the Jews]. Aleteyya, 2020.

Varentsova, I., and G. Shcheboleva. *Anton Chekhov: Dokumenty, Fotografii* [Documents, Photographs]. Sovetskaya Rossiya, 1984.

Yarmolinsky, Avrahm. *Letters of Anton Chekhov*. Viking Press, 1973.

Yarmolinsky, Avrahm. *The Unknown Chekhov: Stories and Other Writings of Anton Chekhov Hitherto Unpublished*. The Noonday Press, 1958.